RICARDO GONZÁLEZ

CONTACT FROM PLANET APU

BEINGS FROM THE FUTURE AMONG US

Luminous Moon Press
Boulder, Colorado

Copyright © 2015 Ricardo González.
All Rights Reserved.

Ricardo González website: www.legadocosmico.com

First English Edition, June 2016
Luminous Moon Press, Boulder, Colorado

Translated from Spanish by Julio Palacio
Edited by Tom Hamblin and Ted Ringer

Illustrations *Antarel* and *Ivika* by Ramiro Rossi
ramirorossi.blogspot.com

Interior & cover design by Carolyn Oakley, Luminous Moon Design
www.luminousmoon.com

No portion of this publication, including the cover design, may be reproduced or used in any form or by any means, electronic or mechanical, including photocopying, recording, or by any information storage and retrieval system, without prior written permission of the publisher and author.

ISBN: 978-0-9968600-3-1

Printed and bound in the United States of America

Dedication

To the inhabitants of the mountain range in Ancash, the first contactees with extraterrestrials from the planet Apu.

To the memory of Vlado Kapetanovic, the first to disseminate information about close encounters with the Apunians: "All for the rest!"

To Paola Harris, Dr. Michael E. Salla, and Georgio Piacenza for helping spread my testimony of contact in the most important circles of English speaking ufology.

To J.J. Benitez, in recognition of his long journey as a journalist and researcher of the "unidentified." His major UFO sighting in Peru, in 1974, was an invitation from an Apunian.

To the memory of Jose Carlos Paz Garcia, founder of IPRI in Peru; his sons Carlos and Sixto; and his daughter, my dear departed friend Rose Marie Paz Wells. They were fundamental to understanding my own experiences. Thank you.

And to Sol, my companion, my strength, my angel.

Table of Contents

Foreword | Extraterrestrial Message for Humanity 11
Michael E. Salla, Ph.D.

Preface 19
Paola Harris

Introduction 21
Ricardo González

The Authentic Extraterrestrial Agenda 25
Ricardo González

1 | Initial Contact 29
    A telepathic message

2 | The Apunians 35
    A "visit" to the Hydroelectric Plant
    The UFOs of Yungay
    An extraterrestrial healing

3 | The Cosmic Plan and Secondary Missions 51
    A greater agenda
    Secondary missions

4 | SCHEDULED SIGHTINGS   59
   The Unidentified seen by journalists
   The legacy of the IPRI
   Our testimony on television
   Sightings by appointment

5 | MOUNT SHASTA AND EXTRATERRESTRIAL BASES   69
   The mountain of contact
   Intraterrestrial city? Apunian base?

6 | INSIDE A SHIP   77
   The experiences can be postponed
   Invitation to a dormant volcano
   The preparation
   Reunion with Antarel

7 | INTERVIEW WITH AN APUNIAN   107
   The Solar Disks
   The extraterrestrial connection to the
      White Brotherhood
   The secret of Altai
   Back at Sand Flat

8 | EXOPOLITICS: THE INVITATION TO MICHAEL SALLA   129

9 | PAOLA HARRIS AND A GROUP CONTACT WITH ANTAREL   137
   Antarel and the threshold of light

10 | HUASCARÁN: APUNIAN BASE   151
   A dream of the "future"
   Ichic Puna
   Llanganuco: Another portal of contact

11 | IVIKA'S MESSAGE — 161
   The Minius
   "We will be one"

Epilogue | TIME — 173

"The Double…" — 177

Contact From Planet Apu

"I believe that these extra-terrestrial vehicles and their crews are visiting this planet from other planets, which obviously are a little more technically advanced than we are here on earth...

"We may first have to show them that we have learned to resolve our problems by peaceful means, rather than warfare, before we are accepted as fully qualified universal team members." –Astronaut Gordon Cooper, Mercury Project

"Time travel poses all sorts of problems, both physical and social..." –Michio Kaku

"If time travel is possible, where are the tourists from the future?" –Stephen Hawking, *A Brief History of Time*

"The difference between the past, present and future is only a persistent illusion." –Albert Einstein

Foreword

Extraterrestrial Message for Humanity

On the weekend of August 3-4, 2013 extraterrestrials delivered an important transformative message for humanity through a workshop led by Peruvian contactee Ricardo González at Mt Shasta, California. Extraterrestrials have come in peace and friendship, and are willing to participate in positive exchanges with humanity. They are willing to support citizen-based forms of galactic diplomacy that will help humanity join the galactic community.

There were approximately 50-55 people attending the workshop being held at Sand Flat, Mt Shasta. All participants were camping. The language of instruction was Spanish, and English translations were provided on an ad hoc basis. Participants were encouraged to film/photograph whatever they witnessed.

Ricardo began by discussing his background. He described his experiences as involving both physical sightings and contacts. He claims his first contact experience was in 1996 at Paititi, Peru with an "intraterrestrial" from an ancient underground civilization. In 1997 he had another contact. This involved meeting a tall Nordic extraterrestrial called Antarel at the Chilca Desert, Peru. Ricardo was taken up into a space ship with Antarel in 2001. He most recent contact was on August 26, 2012 at Mt Shasta. Prior to the contact, a large group of approximately 55 had a physical sighting of a vehicle that did not appear to be a [human made] aircraft or satellite.

The 2012 physical contact occurred after the larger group completed the workshop on the morning of August 26. Ricardo got a psychographic (automatic writing) request to go back to the campsite and, in total, a group of 13 once again had a sighting of what appeared to be an extraterrestrial vehicle. This was another "programed sighting" for a specific time (9:00 pm) that Ricardo had advised a few individuals previously so they could be prepared. Ricardo received another psychographic request to go deeper into the forest by himself. The vehicle projected a ray of light or plasma ball that transported him into a space vehicle for approximately 1.5 hours. When he returned, it seemed that only 15 minutes had elapsed. An English translation of Ricardo's 2012 Contact Report is available at exopolitics.org.

After the introductory session for the 2013 workshop, Ricardo took questions. When I asked how the universal law of attraction applied to contact in terms of positively and negatively inclined humans/ETs, Ricardo said that there were three important considerations that applied here in determining the nature of the contact experiences he is involved with.

Intention has to match. Positive intentions attract positively inclined ETs.

Vibration/Frequency has to match. Generally, this involves human participants raising their consciousness to a level that is compatible with the extraterrestrials.

There has to be an invitation.

These appear to me to be solid principles upon which a respectful form of extraterrestrial contact can occur. It requires a lengthy preparation process during which any individual fears would be overcome.

Ricardo did a number of exercises that helped the group feel comfortable with the possibility of an extraterrestrial sighting or contact. Visualizations were used to achieve this, as well as a silent walk in nature. The environment and energy of Mount

Shasta did provide a unique opportunity to prepare for the unusual. Between exercises, Ricardo and other members of the group took photos of UFOs that appeared.

Ricardo claims that when a UFO pulses a bright light in response to an intention/request, that is a characteristic of an extraterrestrial vehicle. That is different from satellites that pulse during rotation when the sun is reflected at a different angle, and they are generally dimmer. Aircraft are far easier to identify and are always accompanied by the noise from their jet engines.

Prior to the Saturday evening Sky Watch, Ricardo explained that the group would experience what he calls a "programmed sighting," rather than a spontaneous sighting. A "programmed sighting" involves advance notice of when the extraterrestrial vehicle will appear. In the case of the 2013 Mount Shasta workshop, Ricardo had publicly announced a programmed sighting on Chilean TV one month in advance, at which time he also announced that I would be attending. You can watch a video showing Ricardo's televised announcement on exopolitics.org. According to the psychographic communications he received, the sighting would occur between 9-10 pm.

During the sky watch on August 3, Ricardo explained the importance of distinguishing between satellites, aircraft and extraterrestrial vehicles. The latter were brighter and would pulse in response to the group's intentions. The extraterrestrial vehicles came in different sizes according to Ricardo. There are large motherships that ranged in size from several hundred meters to nearly 20 kilometers. There are scoutcraft that are approximately 30 meters in size. There are also probes that are generally two meters in diameter, or even be smaller, that are unmanned.

At 9 pm, the workshop participants were instructed to begin chanting OM, and to continue the chanting throughout the hour. This was done in order to match the vibration/frequency with potential extraterrestrial visitors. With the advance preparation and training, workshop participants immediately began identifying the various objects that were sighted. Aircraft were easily identified, as well as satellites that were very distant and dim. One of the objects at around the 9:10 mark appeared to fulfill the characteristics of an extraterrestrial vehicle. It appeared closer to the earth than a satellite, it pulsed a bright light, and its flight trajectory did not appear to be uniform. Unlike aircraft, there was no jet engine noise. It qualified, according to Ricardo's criteria, as a possible extraterrestrial vehicle, though it was not unambiguous. As the 10 pm mark approached, none of the other 30 or so objects seen appeared to be an extraterrestrial vehicle.

At approximately 9:55, Ricardo asked the audience to be receptive to any messages from extraterrestrials. Soon after, an object moving in a north-easterly direction pulsed a bright red light. It was already near the horizon when it pulsed, so it was a fairly short sighting. Ricardo interpreted it as a sign that the group would receive a message. Ricardo received a message and was beginning to announce it when an object moving from a southerly direction began to glow brightly and gave a very intense pulse.

It was filmed by several participants (two of these are shown in a video on exopolitics.org). It was the most unambiguous demonstration of an extraterrestrial vehicle. Ricardo completed reading the message, and, as if on cue, another object appeared and glowed brightly before delivering another intense pulse of light. It was a second unambiguous demonstration of an extraterrestrial vehicle. Most importantly, it appeared to be confirming the accuracy of the earlier messages received by Ricardo.

Here is the message:

"Yes it is us. You were able to verify our presence in this programmed sighting. We have done it this way to offer our support so that you do not lose the strength to keep going on. The contact with us is real. But more important is our profound relationship with you. We have a message for Michael Salla. We desire that the real reason for our presence reaches more people. This is why it is important that he understands our positive contact intentions and our interest in promoting exchanges with your human society. We will be supporting Michael in this task. The contact has been established. Very important changes are approaching. Be attentive." –Antarel

On the morning of the final day there was a further exercise from Ricardo using visualizations. There was discussion of the Saturday evening sighting and the importance the extraterrestrials attach to preparing the population for contact. Farewells and group photos completed the workshop.

Final Comments

The sky watching on Saturday evening was a remarkable event insofar as there were at least two unambiguous sightings of an extraterrestrial vehicle, with a possible two more. The latter two, which occurred after Ricardo's final message, were captured on video camera. While the night shots are not very clear, it is evidence of two tangible objects in the sky witnessed by 50+ individuals.

It appeared that the sightings also were timed to fulfill the pre-workshop "programed sighting" announcement by Ricardo made on Chilean TV. It is quite an extraordinary phenomenon that a UFO sighting can be announced a month or more in advance, and occur as predicted for the specified time frame.

The "programmed sighting" was successful. Ricardo stressed a relatively rare occurrence for events he is involved with. This event was different insofar as an international extraterrestrial researcher (myself) would be attending.

One important conclusion that can be drawn from the successful "programmed sighting" from the August 2013 workshop is that it supports Ricardo's claim of physical contact occurring at the previous August 2012 Mount Shasta workshop. Ricardo's report of the 2012 physical contact experience contains valuable information about the intentions and activities of the extraterrestrials he works with.

The personal element of the message received by Ricardo during the 2013 programmed sighting came as a surprise to me. The message reveals the importance extraterrestrials attach to the world learning the truth about their visiting our world in peace and friendship. They desire to promote "positive contact" whereby human participants are helped and uplifted by their experiences with extraterrestrial life. Their willingness to conduct exchanges with human society is a sign of the many ways in which they can help humanity to evolve.

The manner in which the workshop was conducted, and the three requirements outlined by Ricardo for contact (1. Intention, 2. Frequency, and 3. Invitation) give confidence that they do have positive intentions for humanity. The emphasis the extraterrestrials (whom Ricardo works with) place on the right preparation of workshop participants, and the respect they show for human free will, does give us confidence to accept their claims.

The feelings evoked by the sightings and the group camaraderie made for an unforgettable event. The personal message from the extraterrestrials does reveal that they value peace and friendship with humanity. Importantly, they are willing to work with private citizens in various exchanges that confirm the significance of citizen-based forms of galactic diplomacy. These possible citizen-based efforts are discussed in my recently published book, *Galactic Diplomacy: Getting to Yes with ET*. The final conclusion is that extraterrestrials involved with the Mount Shasta sighting from 2013 have a transformative message for humanity that inspires hope for a future where humanity is ready to join the galactic community.

Michael E. Salla, Ph.D.
August 9, 2013

Special thanks to Ricardo González and Giorgio Piacenza for their corrections to earlier versions of this Report.

Salla, Michael E. "Extraterrestrial Message for Humanity: Report on Ricardo González Workshop at Mt Shasta." *exopolitics.org*. 09 August 2013

Contact From Planet Apu

Preface

I join Ricardo González in welcoming in a new paradigm for Contact.

Ricardo is a wonderful goodwill ambassador for Extraterrestrial cultures and their messages for planet Earth. He is wise far beyond his years and is able to articulate the history of ancient visitations because of his many travels around the world. Being a researcher, he understands the importance of taking on responsibility and action.

That is where we have something in common. As a UFO investigative journalist and researcher, it took me many years to arrive at the conclusion that part of this phenomenon is spiritually oriented. It was easier for me to remain in the concrete realm, collecting data, recording incidents, interviewing scientists, military personnel, astronauts, pilots and many directly involved with the UFO Phenomena.

There was no common element in the investigations except that it was dimensional. It exists in a non-local realm. It is sometimes a quantum hologram.

But I was not listening. The Phenomena itself was speaking to me as it speaks to many who have been in the field for thirty years as I have. I did not hear the messages. I did not see the light.

It is only when I began going out into the quiet, the desert, the wilderness, the remote places that I began to see another picture. It was only when I retreated from the hectic civilized world that I realized many things. It is only when I began interviewing those who had contact that I began to understand that the Cosmos was addressing the material world, the people of planet Earth.

It was only when I interviewed many Latin American contactees, and Ricardo González was one of them, that I understood that these extraterrestrials were trying to make a "heart connection" with people and it could only be done easily with the peoples of Latin America. Latin American people connect easily and are not solely interested in the craft, and the exotic technologies that powerful Western cultures have copied and back engineered often for "war purposes." These people know how to welcome extraterrestrial beings with open hearts and minds. They look for commonalities, not disparities.

It is now obvious that Contact, as we experience it, is an effort to awaken mankind, to force us to think out of the box, to extend our consciousness to the stars and beyond. It is an exciting new beginning. It is a welcoming of this new paradigm, a new way of thinking that some people call a spiritual technology, a rebirth to who we really are. It is an understanding that we have divine origins and we should strive to humbly get closer to our CREATOR. We need to be reminded.

This is where Ricardo González can so greatly articulate it well. He sees the whole picture 360 degrees. In his travels, he weaves a cosmic tapestry to show the world that we are all ONE! His words make us feel comfortable and very much like returning home.

When we live the experience with him, we see it as a part of reality. It did not seem an alternate reality but a return to our origins. It is an honor to contribute my observations to his book but, most of all, it is an honor to welcome in a new way of seeing this marvelous world, this massive cosmos, this new paradigm. It is wonderful to fly again!

Paola Harris

Introduction

This book took a tremendous turn on April 12, 2015. On that date, I faced a new close encounter with "them." It was an "invitation" to meet at a specific location in the Peruvian Andes of Ancash.

"They," human-looking aliens, wanted to deliver a message and it was blunt and revealing, containing information that has helped us put the loose pieces of the puzzle together—a revelation that completely changed the focus of this book.

Speaking today about the "unidentified" and the possibility of intelligent extraterrestrial life visiting Earth is not as difficult as it was in the 1940s, a decade in which the so-called "modern era of UFOs" began with a sighting by an American pilot, Kenneth Arnold, and the crash of an alleged extraterrestrial object on a ranch in New Mexico. But today, the picture is made more complex by the large amount of information circulating about contact with these beings. This information is presented in TV documentaries that return to the days of Roswell and explore the secrets of an underground military base in Nevada —the mysterious Area 51—gray aliens, abductions and, more recently, "reptilians" and their plot against humanity. All such information goes into the world of conspiracies and has created an "integral theory" about the aliens and their intentions. It is, in my view, partial, sloppy and biased.

This book was originally written to share a different vision of contact with advanced cosmic civilizations: their origin, intentions, approach to humanity and, most importantly, their message. And, as I have said, the special contact in the Peruvian Andes has become a cornerstone guiding the direction of this work.

For over 20 years, I have been contacted by a group of extraterrestrials, that are similar in appearance to us—or perhaps it is we who resemble these "visitors." They differ from humans with their advanced technology and understanding of the universe. They are part of a cluster of highly developed civilizations who have been observing and visiting earth for thousands of years. I am one of many witnesses who claim to have seen them. I even had the opportunity to physically enter their space ships and will explain more regarding this later. Over time, I have learned of their peaceful intentions and ethics, and how important the human race is to the Universe.

Many of the contact experiences with these beings have relied on witnesses and photographic records for validation. On five specific occasions I announced sightings that were scheduled by "appointment" and witnessed by journalists and renowned researchers. In 2013, one such witness was Dr. Michael E. Salla, one of the fathers of the global Exopolitics movement. Salla, along with 55 other witnesses including the Italian-Peruvian ufologist Giorgio Piacenza, a current member of the civilian UFO research committee of the Peruvian Air Force, participated in an interaction with four space ships of non-human origin at the foot of Mount Shasta in the U.S. Dr. Salla, who earned a Ph.D. in Political Science and was a conflict resolution consultant in the Reagan administration, was amazed. And not just by what he saw, but also by what he felt—an energy of fraternity with intelligences from other worlds. In 2014, with more than 160 witnesses from various countries and the renowned journalist and UFO researcher Paola Harris in the lead, we observed and recorded sightings of these objects in the skies over Mount Shasta in a new scheduled meeting. This was a sighting that occurred at the exact time the extraterrestrials had announced. Moreover, seven people experienced direct contact with Antarel, one of the beings who is in communication with us. Paola Harris, herself, was a witness on this occasion. I will talk more about that later.

All these experiences were coordinated with extraterrestrial beings who claim to come from Alpha Centauri, a nearby planet in the constellation of Alpha B. We know these beings as "Apunians." This book is part of their history. There is a process involved with contact. In order to preserve the details of this process, and to understand it in its full context, I decided to include some experiences that were mentioned in previous books. It is important to see the whole picture.

Contact has shaped my life. Through it, I have gained a vision of the universe I did not have before. And, it is the force that encourages me to write this book. To present, once again, a strong and urgent message.

Ricardo González

Contact From Planet Apu

THE AUTHENTIC EXTRATERRESTRIAL AGENDA

For quite a long time we have been visited by advanced cosmic civilizations. Contact with those creatures—many with a humanoid appearance—exceeds UFO research and involves very profound issues. Without a doubt, the one that currently occupies researchers the most is the purpose of these visits and their non-official contact.

Sadly, due to an enormous disinformation campaign, it is believed that these beings' agenda is malignant, a matter of control, in which entities from other worlds infiltrate in our military complexes to collaborate in obscure experiments or unimaginable global domination conspiracies. Although it is true that we can find everything in the Universe and that, in fact, there's an organization behind the shadows interested in controlling the threads of the world, the exaggerated emphasis given to the alleged human-extraterrestrial alliances is a matter of science fiction.

It is ridiculous that beings from other worlds—with the technology and power at their disposal—would need to make deals with military persons in order to transverse the skies with freedom and perform their abductions. Some writers even sustain that there are beings of a reptilian aspect camouflaged as humans. I consider this is part of the game to make the public believe—and also researchers for that matter—that all of that is true. Now, I don't deny that there are different extraterrestrial perspectives regarding humanity but if they had wanted to harm us they would have conquered or eliminated us a long time ago.

I have maintained contacts with human-looking extraterrestrial beings for twenty years. They have allowed us to photograph their spacecraft manifesting during programmed sightings before witnesses. Some of those encounters have taken place before reporters and well-known researchers. I was physically with them on eight occasions and all of those experiences took place in mutual accord.

The main being with whom I have interacted presents himself with the name Antarel. He is a giant measuring almost eight-feet tall, with a Nordic aspect, who communicated mentally. I have always seen him wearing a tight fitting, silver-colored metallic one-piece suit as if it were a second skin. He tells me that they are voyagers in time and in other realities although they are currently settled on a planet close to Alpha Centauri, some 4.2 light years away from Earth. He has also spoken to me about advanced civilizations in the Orion, Pleiades and Canis Major (Sirius) sectors.

Antarel affirms that they are part of an extraterrestrial organization which has noble assistance purposes. They do not manifest openly because they follow strict protocols of action. This organization is known as "The Confederation" and, according to Antarel, this confederation imposed a quarantine of protection for Earth since the 1940s. This was due to the fact that during those years we produced dangerous actions that sent a signal to the Universe, a signal that could attract extraterrestrial creatures of a more scientific and military condition. Our main actions were the Philadelphia Experiment in 1943 (in which we opened a space-time crease that exposed us) and the atomic bombs over Japan in 1945.

For that reason, two years after the Second World War ended, UFO sightings increase and the Roswell Incident take place. According to Antarel, that craft was downed by the Confederation.

In the 1950s the witness contact testimonies with extraterrestrials involved beings sent by the Confederation, beings who were elected by their close resemblance to human beings. But when the military began to research—and to misinform—about contacts with extraterrestrials, a greater emphasis was given to abduction cases.

After the 1961 abduction episode experienced by the (Betty and Barney) Hill marriage—an event that was detracted upon and sensationalized—researchers of the UFO phenomenon focused only upon those kinds of experiences. The conspiracies, the malignant grey agenda, and so on, has dominated the North American UFO scene for decades and that which it entails is but a small portion of the truth. Furthermore, it is a small and highly manipulated fragment. Someone is interested in fostering fear in relation to contacts with extraterrestrials.

In Latin America, perhaps due to being born in a different cultural context and distant from that tendentious information, the contact with emissaries of the Confederation continued and they, as always, have provided positive messages that include alternatives and hope.

They say that our humanity will become part of a Cosmic Community. That is one of the reasons why they don't intervene openly. They are evaluating us. They want to see if they can trust in us. We are not an experiment in the literal sense someone might interpret upon reading these words. In truth, we are their descendants and we are their past and their future. Their existence and ours are connected. For that reason they patiently observe us, waiting for the unraveling.

We have to keep in mind that the perception of time in these beings is quite different from that of (Earth) human beings. For us thousands of years have transpired since they were here, for instance during pre-dynastic times in Egypt. However, for them that event took place "last week." They have seen us grow, make mistakes, stand up once more and, after all that time observing us, they say that there is more good than evil in the world. The thing is that "evil" is more publicized.

That is the reason why I write these words to you. Extraterrestrial contact is vaster and more complex than what is normally broadcast.

In the end we will understand that the true close encounter we wanted to reach wasn't with *them* but with ourselves.

It is time to bring this message of hope closer to all.

Ricardo González

Chapter 1

Initial Contact

I have told my story many times. Especially before television cameras, where the focus was on my gestures, while I said, "Yes, I've had close encounters with extraterrestrials." Regardless of the country or form of media, reporters always listened with both interest and skepticism.

Point blank they asked me how it all began.

I explained that, although I have had a relationship with these beings since my childhood in Lima, it wasn't until my teens that the "formal" contact began to occur.

Today, as I write these lines, I have just turned 41 years old, yet I remember those early experiences as if they happened yesterday.

My first UFO sightings occurred in the mountain town of Chosica, gateway to the Andes, located in a district of Lima. Chosica is known for its hiking trails and picnic areas. It is also the sole travel route to the falls known as the San Pedro Palacala waterfalls, that sit at the foot of the mysterious Marcahuasi mountain. I first saw the first "walking light," as I called it then, in the skies of Chosica. As a child who watched the starry night, a privilege in the city of Lima, I observed satellites almost all year. However, these particular "satellites" stopped and made zigzags or made sudden changes in direction.

In 1988, at the age of 14, I was living with my parents in the district of San Miguel on a road that led to the airport. Being close to the airport, I was used to seeing planes and many other typical aircraft. It was at that time, while standing in the yard outside my home, that I witnessed something that would ultimately alter my understanding of the world: It was a large, luminous, silent object – in full daylight. Amazed, I saw a sphere that appeared almost like a drop of water, very bright in its center with dim light around the edges, making no noise as it traveled toward the Pacific Ocean. I watched with a bewildered sense of joy, as if my inner self knew what it was. A few days later, on radio and television, there was talk of widespread UFO sightings in the country. I was not alone in seeing this object.

I learned that the term "UFO" meant "Unidentified Flying Object," an acronym coined by the United States Air Force during the late 1940s. What were these UFOs? Secret military ships? And, if they were secret military ships, why were they in Peru? Had I seen an extraterrestrial vehicle? And if so, why me? A small boy in a third-world country.

It is important to note that I come from an ordinary family that had no interest in anything unidentified, although my father, who worked for many years as an IT officer in the Peruvian Department of Social Security had a strong interest in the mysterious and the unknown. This was evident from his collection of books on ancient Egypt, mythology and Eastern esotericism. My mother worked in one of the branches of the bank Bancoper. She was not as interested in these issues as my father was. She was very Catholic and deeply religious. She was, nonetheless, happy and perhaps this is why she kept me enrolled at the Marist Brothers primary school in Barranco. However, I had trouble assimilating into a formal education full of rules, and this motivated my parents to move me to another school with a different approach. So, I ended up attending the Walt Whitman School with its intensive English program and a more casual teaching style. Here, I attended high school and learned music, learning to play the guitar and keyboards.

It was during this period that I decided to change my dream of becoming a cartoonist or painter to that of a musician. My music teacher, the great pianist Concho Stuffs, thought I would be a good composer. But that part of my personal history would develop an unexpected "twist," as if it was a masterstroke of fate to guide me into contact with extraterrestrial beings. Later, my training would help me write the music for the Mintaka[1] project. My younger siblings, José Luis and Mariella would find their professions without much difficulty. In my case, at the end of college, although I was excited about music, I started studying marketing at the Peruvian Institute of Marketing and afterwards worked for several years in the pharmaceutical industry. I share these personal details to show that we were, and still are, a normal family. My life followed a normal course in spite of my UFO experiences, including the significant UFO sighting in 1988. The 1988 sighting was impressed upon my mind as an extraordinary unexplained experience. However, as I said, in my heart I knew that there was something else. Still, I let it go.

Until October of 1993, when *they* returned, and even more powerfully.

A telepathic message

In October of 1993, I was 19 years old, and I was studying for a statistical accounting course. While studying, I certainly did not have UFOs on my mind, when suddenly, fatigue overcame me and I decided to take a break, closed my eyes and let my body relax, as much as it, could on the hard chair.

"Be sure to keep looking," I heard a strange and calm voice say in my head. This voice sounded like that of a young man, and was communicating with me in a friendly manner. I was stunned. And I was reluctant to believe it.

"We are extraterrestrial beings and we are contacting you," added the strange mental voice.

Then, to my surprise, he concluded his message by saying, *"You will be given preparation so that you can meet us physically."*

I truly could not believe it.

Had many hours of study and fatigue induced me to imagine all this? Even though I always suspected that we were not were alone in the Universe, I was awake and I was receiving a telepathic message from an alleged extraterrestrial being. It was overwhelming.

Then I answered, "I need something that can prove this is real."

And the voice in my head surprisingly responded, *"Come up to the roof of your house, and there you will see us."*

"This is impossible," I thought. "Now what do I do?"

Having nothing to lose, I decided to go up to the terrace of our apartment in Orrantia del Mar. I convinced my brother Pepe to accompany me, not knowing what would happen. He followed me to see what was happening. This would be an important night for both of us.

"A UFO! A UFO! That light is moving!" We looked at each other in disbelief.

And indeed, a dense red light, which at first appeared to be an antenna, began to move in our direction. As it approached, I could see that the object was a triangular shape with a curvilinear structure, resembling a boomerang. It briefly overshadowed us and then returned the way it had come, toward the Andes.

Hearing our excitement, my parents and sister, Mariella, climbed to the rooftop to see what was happening. From this vantage point, they also saw the foreign object. It left slowly, without making any sound. All of us saw it.

During this magic moment, and through all the excitement, I heard again a mental voice that said something like this: *"We come with good intentions. As we've proceeded with you today, we've done before with other people, and we will continue to do in the future so that they will become aware of our presence.*

"You will not only be contacted by us; there are also other beings that are waiting."

At the time, I didn't know what this meant.

The silence was deafening as we watched the UFO disappear into the misty skies above Lima. As in 1988, these unidentified appearances increased and, ultimately, forced the press to pay attention. This was the beginning of contact with *them*.

This unusual afternoon was the first of a chain of events that occurred over time to postpone my becoming a musician. It seemed my plans for the future had suddenly changed.

At just nineteen years old, I began to examine all the strange things that had happened in my life. I began to realize that everything seems to happen for a reason.

In time, I learned that this communication was coming from a being named, Antarel, who was from the planet, Apu. I would meet him, physically, later, but first some history.

---

[1] www.planetabenítez.com

Contact From Planet Apu

Chapter 2

THE APUNIANS

As you can imagine, these early encounters with Antarel, through telepathic messages and corroborated sightings, took me in a new direction and my life has never been the same. After a series of synchronistic events, I began to participate in investigative groups focusing on extraterrestrial contact. There I learned that, since the 1950s, there have been a number of *close encounters* in Peru with travelers from Apu, Antarel's home planet.

In an effort to understand my own experience, one of the first cases I investigated was one that took place in Ancash, in the beautiful mountains of the Huaylas, in west central Peru.

The Ancash history is very rich. It is linked to the earliest cultures of ancient Peru, from 13,000 BC with the development of the Lithic and Archaic traditions progressing to the influence of the Caral-Supe civilization. Moreover, the Ancash is the cradle of the mysterious Chavin culture, which later influenced the Recuay and Wari cultures, which developed into the Inca Empire and remained intact until the time of the Spanish conquest.

In those early years of contact, I visited the Huascarán National Park and the restricted area of the Huayhuash Mountain Range. I also visited the archaeological site of the aforementioned Chavin: a stone temple nestled at an altitude of 10,423 feet, famous for its complex network of roads and underground galleries. In ancient times, these were illuminated by light admitted through strategically placed ducts. Inside the temple, through this natural light, you can see the Lanzón monolith, a strange, carved anthropomorphic stone deity, almost fifteen feet in height.

Above: the Lanzón monolith.

Many UFO sightings, throughout the Andean region, have been reported as far back as the 1950s. Perhaps the most famous case occurred in 1960 and involved Vlado Kapetanovic, an electrician who worked at the Central Huallanca hydroelectric plant. Vlado encountered a human-looking alien, who brought a message of peace. Vlado's experience was very similar to my contact with Antarel. In fact, it had the same source—the Apunians.

A "visit" to the Hydroelectric Plant

Kapetanovic was born about 1918 in Kolasin, Montenegro. After the Second World War, he came to work as a technician at the Huallanca hydro facility in the Peruvian Andes. There, he had his first contact.

The plant is located in a tunnel, under 374 feet of rugged mountain terrain. On Thursday, March 10, 1960, there was a power outage a little after midnight. Kapetanovic, in charge, went to discover the source of the problem Emergency generators were located outside the tunnel, so he went to them to turn them on. In the midst of this task, he was surprised by a bright light that lit up the surrounding darkness, as if it were day.

The light came from a disk-shaped device which rested on a piece of land near the confluence of the Santa and Quitaracsa rivers, about 1300 feet away. Vlado said the object was supported by solid light beams, in contact with the ground. That is to say, the object appeared weightless, half a meter above the ground. He, then, saw the crew of the ship. They looked very human, though taller.

The crew approached him and spoke in his own language, Yugoslavian.

Several of Kapetanovic's fellow workers had experienced similar visits and told him, very calmly, not to be alarmed. They assured him that the beings were friends and that they had cured many people of the Andean town from numerous illnesses. They were called Apunians.

Apu, as these beings would tell Kapetanovic in future meetings, was the name of their home world. A similar sounding word in the Quechua language means "mountain" or "sir." Was this meaningful? Did this have any relationship to the world of origin of these extraterrestrial beings? Was it describing their home as a mountainous planet? Was this why they were here in this mountainous area?

Vlado didn't believe that this encounter was with extraterrestrials. He thought, because of the horrors he lived through in the Second World War, that this must be a secret post-war mission of Nazi Germany.

"At first," Vlado said, "I didn't think these tall, blonde people were extraterrestrials. With my memories of the war, I thought they were spies of some nation with advanced military prototypes and that they were chasing me, for some unknown reason. In fact, I reported it to a local police station. But then, with all of the psychic, telepathic and technological demonstrations they gave me, I ended up convinced that they were not of this world..."

In this first contact, the Apunians told him they were not Germans, and clarified that they had not intentionally caused the blackout on the ground. However, the presence of their space ship certainly had something to do with it and his data corroborated the fact. Vlado later learned that another incident in Chimbote had generated a power outage in Huallanca. After that brief conversation, the extraterrestrials left, but visited Kapetanovic in future meetings.

Vlado died in Peru in 2005. I met him in person, at a conference on UFOs in Lima. He was a man of strong character, but friendly and humble, who was elated to have spoken with our Apunian brothers. Vlado's experiences were presented as fiction in several books under his pen name, Vitko Novi.[1]

Unfortunately, Vlado's telling of the encounters with the Apunians also contained his own ideas and worldview. Vlado controversially attributed the Apunians as having incarnated as figures in human history, including Jesus. There were other claims Vlado made which, unfortunately, diminished his credibility. However, if we stick with the testimony and facts, Vlado's experience was nonetheless very important because it gave us a record of the ongoing Apunian contact that had occurred for many years with the men of the Andean Ancash.

Although Vitko Novi was the first to write openly about these Apunian encounters, he was not the first to be contacted by them. In the mountains of Yungay, the humble inhabitants of villages in the White Mountain Range had, for some time, already been in communication with the *spacemen*.

The UFOs of Yungay

As if the contact at the hydroelectric plant was not enough, Kapetanovic, in another meeting with the Apunians in the 1960s, was told of an impending disaster at Yungay, which, in fact, did occur ten years later.

According to Vlado, he had observed what he called a time screen, inside their space ship. The Apunians, using peculiar time and dimensional management capabilities, had shown him an avalanche that buried many people after a massive earthquake in that area. Vlado informed the authorities – including a Justice of the Peace – of this upcoming event well in advance, but no one believed him. The local authorities

---

[1] Among the many books published in Peru, *Apu, A World Without Money,* and *170 Hours with Extraterrestrials,* describes Vlado's experiences with the Apunians.

were aware of the stories about extraterrestials in the Andean communities. "Those *cholos*[2] are talking nonsense," the officials of Yungay would contemptuously respond.

The tragedy occurred on May 31, 1970. A 7.8 magnitude earthquake, with its epicenter in the Pacific Ocean, shook Ancash and was felt in almost all of Peru.

It was 3:23 pm when, without warning, more than 20,000 residents of the small town of Yungay disappeared. The release of a huge block of snow and ice from the eastern peak of Mount Huascarán produced a violent avalanche, just as the Apunians had shown Kapetanovic.

The strong quake, which lasted only 45 seconds, wiped out not only Yungay, but also small neighboring villages in the district of Ranrahirca. It was estimated that the death toll reached 80,000 people, with another 20,000 unaccounted for. The total number of injured was recorded to be around 143,331, with the number affected to be more than three million people.

Would the extraterrestrials have been able to prevent this tragedy?

They had tried to warn of the tragedy, but were unable to specify the exact day or month of the earthquake. Nonetheless, they had accurately anticipated the seismic event and its consequences.

Over the passing years, I have come to realize that these beings have many limitations in regard to their involvement in our affairs; at least, those who come with friendly intentions and respect for our free will. Still, within those limitations of nonintervention they informed Kapetanovic that a disaster would occur in Yungay. Unfortunately, the warnings were not heeded. Even a few years before the catastrophe,

---

[2] A derogatory term for people with mixed Latin American and Amerindian descent

Above: Yungay, "before and after" the avalanche that buried it.

Yungay was stunned by an intense wave of UFOs. It was as if the extraterrestrials were trying to get the attention of the townspeople. This was captured and recorded in photographs in 1967 (see photo page 44). If it is not fraud, then they are the best pictures of unidentified objects in the UFO history of Peru.

The Spanish journalist, J.J. Benitez, has kindly allowed me to publish his investigation of that case.

> "According to my information, these images came as follows:

> "One day in March, Augusto Arrandas visited the small town of Yungay in the Ancash Mountains. Before leaving

for the excursion, he asked his friend Cesar Oré, a resident of the same town and employee in the office of Tourism, to borrow a 40-year-old Voightlander camera. He bought a roll of film and it was his friend Ore who was in charge of loading the camera, since Arranda did not quite understand how to operate the camera.

"Augusto left Yungay, willing to tour some of the stunning surrounding mountains, such as the infamous 'Alley of Huaylas' which was whipped in 1970 by the most violent earthquake in the history of Peru. Its summit rises nearly 4,000 meters [13,123 feet] and provides a splendid panorama.

"It was in these mountains that Arranda saw and photographed UFOs and then shared his experience with Oré.

"On his return to Lima, after developing the roll of film, Arranda sent a sealed photo album to Yungay with copies of the pictures of the peaks and UFOs. Some photos, which included the UFO pictures at the end of the album, remained 'forgotten' at his house for two years.

"Everything would have been lost in the earthquake if it were not for the American researcher J. Richard Greenwell. In 1968, copies of some of the photos indirectly fell into Richard's hands.

Due to this 'coincidence' – or non 'coincidence'? – an investigation was launched that allowed everyone to learn of an amazing turn of events.

"Greenwell noted that, after some investigation, the photographs were found at the Peruvian Kodak

Laboratory. There, an employee of the company, violating the rules of the company, kept copies of the UFO sequence. The Kodak managers confiscated the photos of the employee before Richard Greenwell could locate them. These Peruvian executives, the American researcher recounted, refused to provide the copies to him. But in 1969, Greenwell was able to acquire them through Eastman Kodak's International Market. (Mercados Internacionales de Eastman Kodak) in Rochester, New York.

"The location of a complete set of photographs in Yungay was made possible by an official of the Peruvian Marine Ministry (Ministerio de Marina del Peru). Greenwell traveled to Yungay and was able to meet with Mr. Oré, who provided copies of all three missing photos, which had been held in Lima by Peruvian Kodak, Inc. Greenwell was tying up loose ends, making four copies that apparently form the entire sequence."[3]

Photographs from 1967 (see next page) show extraordinary objects in the skies above the village. If these photographs are authentic, then we are seeing Apunian ships in Yungay three years before the earthquake. Kapetanovic, as I said, was the first contactee who spoke publicly about the extraterrestrials of Apu. As he explained, these were extraterrestrials who were space travelers, who had lost their home world and, later, established themselves elsewhere in the cosmos – in the stellar region of Alpha Centauri. At some point, they established underground bases on Earth. In addition, there are other cases of contact with

---

[3] www.planetabenitez.com

Contact From Planet Apu

Above: Two scanned photographs of the mysterious Yungay UFOs (1967).

these spacemen, other reports of their presence in the Andean region of Ancash.

An extraterrestrial healing

In 1970, the year of the terrible earthquake and landslide in Yungay, another person, from the mountains of Ancash, also claimed to have entered into communication with extraterrestrials. Perhaps it was the same extraterrestrial who contacted Kapetanovic. This contactee was Donato Cervantes, a humble man from Huaraz, who worked as a mechanic, driver and farmer. According to his account, on September 14 of that year, he had his first UFO encounter while driving on the Pan-American highway. This occurred while he was traveling toward Huaraz, at a place called Monte Grande (Big Mountain). Donato saw a very bright light on top of a hill. There, he found an object that emitted a strange buzzing, which he *heard* in his head. This was the beginning of his telepathic contact with beings that later appeared to him. They were tall men, over two meters tall and Nordic-looking. They seemed to be the same extraterrestrials from Apu who, a decade earlier, were reported by Kapetanovic. Like the Apunians who contacted the Yugoslav, Donato Cervantes was convinced they were extraterrestrials and learned later that they possessed extraordinary healing powers. In 1983, Cervantes was healed by the extraterrestrials after cutting his arm in a car accident.

Donato relates that it was a deep wound; he made a tourniquet and then, in shock, drove for hours, leaving it untreated. Subsequently, his arm developed gangrene. The doctors advised him that he should have come sooner to the specialized center. His arm was injured to a point where the doctors could no longer save it. Hence, without giving Donato a choice, they were going to amputate his arm on June 17, 1983, in the Central Hospital of Huaraz. This was the case until, the big brothers of the cosmos, as he called them, intervened.

On June 16, one day before the amputation, the extraterrestrials telepathically asked Donato to stay in a hotel and to wait there to be healed. Donato followed the instruction and, indeed, that night the spaceship appeared, throwing off an intense light, concentrated on his arm. From that moment on, he felt no more discomfort. Later, when he returned to the hospital, the amazed doctors found that the arm of this humble Andean driver had been completely healed. There was now no need to perform the operation. In the Huaraz Central Hospital archives, there is documentation of Cervantes arm injury and his apparently miraculous recovery. As if that were not enough, extraterrestrial healing affected Donato's arm with a unique side effect – any sound near his right hand was transmitted on the radio. Randomly and incredibly, Donato was now broadcast on radio frequencies, surprising many radio stations. This occurred unexpectedly as he was talking to his wife, or playing

Above: The June 25, 1984 issue of *Extra*, reporting about Donato Cervantes and his amazing healing. Apunians?

the *charango*, (a small musical instrument, similar to a guitar) that he loved.

On August 28, 2013, at 71 years old, Donato Cervantes began to reconnect with those beings who had never revealed their origin. They said only that they were outsiders who came from the stars, from a celestial galaxy. It was the X9 galaxy that Kapetanovic said was the native home of the extraterrestrials from Apu.

Above: The phenomenon of radio waves emitted by the hand of Cervantes is published by the newspaper *Chronicle*, April 17, 1984.

In 1974, fourteen years after the Kapetanovic case, the Peruvian brothers Carlos and Sixto Paz Wells also came into contact with the Apunians. Thus, Antarel, Sordaz, Godar and other Apunians were in communication with the now disbanded investigative group Rama: An important contact movement that existed as an organization until 1991. Despite its "official" dissolution, Rama's members have continued to be active in various Latin American countries. It is very clear that the "outreach program that began in Peru in the 1950s in the Andes of Ancash had gone to a different stage, involving multiple witnesses or, in short, a group of contactees. Since late 1993, I have joined and participated in the collective process of that contact. It was there I learned that these encounters with extraterrestrials were a program or agenda to integrate human beings into a cosmic community. The same star family to which Antarel and the Apunians belong. As happened with the Rama group in 1974, I found several testimonies of contact with Apunians in various countries for example the Aztlan Group in Spain, now dissolved. Clearly, the Apunians had a different agenda, which was not tied to any one group.

Through these ongoing contacts, we have learned why that civilization in Alpha Centauri has been so interested in contacting us. *They* have wanted to warn us of something very sobering.

In those early years of contact with the Apunians, I learned that they were not only amazingly evolved technologically, they were also super psychic, as Kapetanovic had reported. In fact, Antarel and his associates, called themselves extraterrestrial guides, a kind of mental doctors. It was their intention to help us and it was they who suggested that our training should be based on relaxation, concentration, and meditation techniques.

As I immersed myself in all this, I continued to learn more. I managed to intiate the telepathic contact with Antarel and was able to arrange scheduled sightings on the beach in Chilca and in the Marcahuasi mountains. However, despite this training and my intentions to relate more with the extraterrestrials, it was very clear that it was they who decided when, where, and how contact was to occur. Vlado's experience was similar—it was the Apunians who decided.

Ricardo González

It wasn't easy to cope with all this. While it was beautiful and revealing, this was also a completely different understanding of reality. I tried to personally deal with these experiences and still balance my daily responsibilities. I was working for an international firm where I did not talk about extraterrestrials in the hallways. However, invitations to speak about this topic at conferences and in interviews in Peru and abroad began to multiply and my colleagues in the office began to learn about these other activities.

All my presentations on this topic were free. I had a job with a good salary, so I covered all of the necessary costs for my speaking engagements. However, the time eventually came when I could not afford it entirely.

I had my first *physical* encounter with Antarel on August 30, 1997. That contact occurred in the desert of Chilca, about nine miles into the mountains. It was in the same area where J.J. Benitez had seen two UFOs. (In 1974 he had an encounter with an extraterrestrial named Kulba Apu, which was arranged through a message received by Carlos Paz Wells.) My first physical meeting with Antarel was intense. I immediately recognized him as the telepathic speaker who had contacted me years earlier.

The Apunians, as I mentioned, have an average height of two meters, but Antarel was one of the tallest at 8.8 feet tall. A true giant. He had the appearance of a 35 year-old athlete with Nordic features and slanted eyes. He wore a silver metal suit, attached to his body, as if it were a second skin. In subsequent contacts, where I could be closer to him, I saw that his eyes were honey-colored and were highlighted against his impeccable white skin. He had very fine platinum blonde hair, almost gray, and of shoulder length. His appearance was so beautiful that if

I had seen him thousands of years ago, I would have thought that he was an angel.

In my first contact with Antarel in the Peruvian desert and, as told in my book *Cosmic Legacy*[4], I was invited to physically climb into one of their space ships. At the time, this invitation scared me and I could barely face the situation that I was presented with.

However, Antarel sincerely reassured me, through a telepathic message, that they would wait until I was ready to meet them aboard their vehicles.

I never imagined I would enter their ships not once, but twice.

---

[4] *El Legado Cósmico,* Cecosami, Lima, 2002.

Chapter 3

The Cosmic Plan and Secondary Missions

I recall those intense years with great emotion. We were a group of young people, who gathered nearly every weekend, in the desert or in the mountains, training to experience contact. Other kids our age looked at us suspiciously and asked if we were part of a religion or belonged to a cult. They couldn't believe that we would leave the delights of Lima to waste time with meditation practices, under the canopy of stars at Marcahuasi Chilca.

For us, it was a beautiful experience with or without extraterrestrial contact. There we learned a lot about ourselves. We began to understand our fears and emotions and become comfortable in the silence. We also studied what happened in the sky to help us avoid confusion about the things we witnessed. We learned that the Iridium constellation of sixty-six communication satellites reflect sunlight off of their panels and are easily mistaken for stars. The ISS (International Space Station) is the size of a football field. There are many objects in the night sky that, in fact, are man-made. As impressive as it is, this human technology is often mistaken by witnesses as genuine UFO sightings. Those unforgettable nights in the desert and in the mountains allowed us to see with our eyes and to be able to tell the difference. We also got to marvel at the presence of the spaceships.

Today, having lived the experience of contact, those of us who were there are confident that a significant percentage of unidentified objects that are reported today as abnormal are, in fact, alien spacecraft. In Chilca, there were amazing demonstrations of these phenomena. We saw objects travel in triangular formations, which then broke ranks and shot off in different directions. They did so with great speed, traveling outward as if to mingle with the stars. We saw what looked like constellations, only to witness these seemingly static stars move. Once we saw six to seven ships stationed motionlessly above us and then witnessed them rearrange themselves. There was a lot that our astronomy did not know.

These objects have shed silver strands of material, which reached the ground and fell onto our camp. In these experiences, astonishingly, we witnessed or experienced "light" as a solid, because we could touch it with our hands. We felt a great camaraderie of cosmic brotherhood with our visitors. These demonstrations became, for us, proof of contact.

Once we became more sure of what we were experiencing, we began to understand the message that aliens were conveying to us. But there were many questions. How long have they been coming? Why is mankind so important to them? Why don't they show themselves openly? Why were we young Peruvians, in a country with no great political importance, experiencing all of this? And, exactly what was their message?

Antarel, and other extraterrestrial beings who have come into contact with countless witnesses in Peru, have been sharing, little by little, scenes of a cosmic history that have been very difficult to digest. It sounds like science fiction, but if everything they've told us is true, the visits from these beings are of great importance and meaning.

Ricardo González

A greater agenda

It isn't easy to summarize such an extraordinary story[1].

The Apunians claim that the universe contains multiple dimensions, worlds, and intelligent civilizations. Each of these realities involve different levels of consciousness. On the huge universal stage, there exist extraterrestrial civilizations that have preceded us, who have reached a very high level of technological development. However, some of them have become highly cerebral and technologically focused and have lost touch with their emotions. They have become arrested in their process of evolution. This has led these civilizations to understand that they must return to their origins. In this process, human beings play a "mirror" role, assisting others in remembering who they are, acting as a guide in their steps so that they might recover their true direction.

But this process isn't random. The appearance of human beings is part of a project to seed a new way of life to assist in a new synthesis of the existing universe. Working together, a link is created allowing the universe to continue to grow. The earth and humans are part of that process that the extraterrestrials call the Cosmic Plan.

According to the extraterrestrial guides, this Master Project has three basic components:

1. *Where to carry out the project.* This dictates relocating a "dead planet" to an alternate reality and ultimately restoring life to it through a parallel dimension. According to these beings, such was the case with the Earth, which had at one time been devastated by the impact of a catastrophic meteoric

---

[1] In my book *Nuestros Lazos Extraterrestres (Our Extraterrestrial Connections)*, (Ecis Publications, Buenes Aires, 2004) I discuss this cosmic history.

shower. Supposedly, it was more than 1.2 billion years ago. According to them, to rescue Earth, a group of extraterrestrial scientists—from somewhere in the Pleiades star system—made a trip back in time, reaching our planet before it was destroyed. They created from that moment on, a parallel reality to the future—a kind of space-time paradox where our world might survive and, later, house humans. As I write these lines, the "alternate timeline" which was long ago activated for the Earth so that it would have a future with humans, is being cast in real time with the universe. That is, we will exist in the matrix from which the extraterrestrials have come. That matrix being an array of "multiple dimensions."

Our "insertion," which began after December 21, 2012, coincides with the end of the Mayan Calendar and represents major changes in extraterrestrial civilizations' Long Count. It is a long and gradual process already underway. It is a process that the beings of the cosmos symbolically call, Third Time.

2. *To promote the lifestyle project.* Secured to a new parallel reality, life will be planted on the "rescued" planet. By assisting nature, the best framework for the development of the species is established. At its inception, this involved, in the case of earth, the genetic modification of ancient anthropoids at the hands of a group of extraterrestrial minds. These great minds, as I previously mentioned and, according to the account of the guides, come from the Pleiades star system. Through this process, the humans, or Homo Sapiens, were born and became the black race. The "intervention" occurred in Africa, in a place that many esoteric texts associate with the lost world of Lemuria.

3. *Nuturing the lifestyle project.* As part of this enormous learning and development plan, the extraterrestrials would foster, on Earth, the gradual integration of knowledge. Thus, they germinated the first great civilizations of our world, most of which are yet unknown to us.

However, there was a breakdown in this process. The extraterrestrials found that their presence generated dependency upon them and, for this reason they decided to leave, allowing the human beings to rediscover for themselves their own merit and their original mission. According to Antarel, at this stage there was a lot of interference from other extraterrestrial civilizations that did not take kindly to the human mission acting as a bridge with the universe. These alien disputes are well reflected in legends and texts of the ancient Egyptian and Sumerian cultures. Currently, various civilizations of the cosmos are watching us with keen interest, since whatever mankind may achieve, it will have an impact on them and their worlds of origin.

Secondary missions

The agenda of these differently organized civilizations, acting on our perceived material plane, obey a superior design of consciousness issued by non-physical universes. which require the application of different programs to affect the Earth. The intention was to create working groups that were connected to the emissaries, extraterrestrials serving the Cosmic Plan. These additional side missions, although in line with the Master Plan, had their specific objectives, phases and stages of implementation. For the extraterrestrials, it was also a sort of anthropological approach involving humans that could be measured to see how we responded to contact experiences. The experience with groups in Peru was one of these side quests.

Above: The Chilca desert in Peru, the setting the extraterrestrials chose to prepare contact groups.

The program, according to the extraterrestrials, had four phases of preparation, which, according to my understanding, standardizes any exchange involving beings from other worlds:

1. *Aurón* or The call of contact.
2. *Xendra* or Experiences of contact.
3. *Lunar* or Receiving information.
4. *Xolar* or Distribution of the acquired knowledge.

The process makes sense. It first involves a "call" which gives an individual the powerful feeling that they are part of something very real. This is followed by a concrete contact experience that highlights the visit of these beings and their intentions to connect with us. Once the connection is established, a third phase emerges: the exchange of knowledge. They learn from humans—our feelings, dreams and actions. The humans, in turn, receive important insights into cosmic history, although this may occur gradually. All this unfolds according to the level of individual consciousness and how advanced the individual is on their path. It is this understanding that precedes the fourth phase: a sharing or radiating of the knowledge we have acquired. In other words, the time comes when we begin to radiate with knowledge just as the sun radiates energy.

While the extraterrestrials involve themselves in secondary missions among us, each of them pursue specific objectives and tasks integrated into the Master Plan, which seeks the insertion of our world into a "cosmic community" as defined by the American astronaut Edgar Mitchell[2].

As I mentioned earlier, since the end of 2012, and, not coincidentally, by the end of the Mayan calendar, Long Count extraterrestrial secondary missions have begun to merge with the parent program, meaning the Cosmic Plan. Therefore, a new cycle has been initiated where rapprochement with space beings should be viewed with a different vision. A review of extraterrestrial interactions is important in order to understand the mission of the Apunians amid a general plan, agreed upon by different civilizations in our galaxy.

Of course, the experience with different contact witnesses and groups in our world has been very important to extraterrestrials in order to study human reactions to interactions with more advanced cosmic societies. For that reason, in addition to scientific or military interaction, they have also contacted witnesses from the general population. They needed to know if they could trust us, and also if we dared to trust them. In fact,

---

[2] Edgar Mitchell was a renowned astronaut, lunar module pilot of the Apollo 14 mission and the sixth man to walk on the moon. Mitchell repeatedly complained that NASA and the U.S. government have hidden information about extraterrestrial visitation.

it was important that those witnesses, who were brave enough, share their testimony of contact, unlike other witnesses from religious, military or scientific fields, who have been elusive or silent on the subject.

In my case, after I shared my experience with the news media as one of those witnesses, my whole life was upended and had changed forever.

Even then, in the mid-1990s in Lima, the extraterrestrials had asked me if I was willing to devote myself full time to spreading the message they were communicating to me. Delivered from my heart, my answer was a resounding yes. It was 1998, when they told me that my time had finally come. They announced the upcoming planned sighting of their ships to take place over the skies of Peru in January, 1999. This amazing sighting was filmed and led me to appear on Peruvian national television to speak about it with reporters. Weeks after my appearance, I was fired from my job.

I had begun another stage in my path.

Chapter 4

SCHEDULED SIGHTINGS

Everything was magical. I do not believe in coincidences, but it was as if each step had been planned to the last detail.

We had been told, but then it really happened. A wave of sightings shook Peru. It was a statement, an announcement, by the Apunians, in order to accustom the public to contact.

A message reached me in mid-October 1998, first through dreams, and then through one particular telepathic communication that manifested through automatic writing.

When I experience this type of communication, I receive a feeling, a mental rush of energy, that contains data and information. This is accompanied by the desire and ability to write out this information. I keep all of these communications in a special notebook. The messages are perfectly articulated and flow in native language. It should be clarified that these kinds of experiences feel good, because when the communication occurs I experience a deep sense of calm and connection. I must stress that this telepathic connection with the extraterrestrials has nothing to do with other phenomena that are associated with mediumship. In the messages I have received, I have always been aware of the incoming transmissions accompanied by this sense of peace and wellbeing.

Through this means of contact, the extraterrestrials alerted me to an unprecedented wave of UFOs that would shake Peru, the most intense and prolonged one experienced, so far, in my country. The highlight of this wave of programmed sightings was the testimony of the national press: Journalists became key chroniclers of the presence of the ships. Although I mentioned this incident in other publications, I consider it necessary to briefly review the event for the reader, putting into context the contact that later occurred with the Apunians on Mount Shasta.

The Unidentified seen by journalists

Among the previously received psychographic messages and sightings that began on January 22, 1999 in Peru, I quote these two important statements:

"1999 will be the year of evidence, and we will support you with our events captured by both you and the news media..."
–Oxalc, November 24, 1998

"As in 1993, 1995 and 1996, our ships will be strong in Peru, as well as in several key locations worldwide. This is to further sensitize the human mind before our visit. Thus, we plan to give them evidence of our presence so that they understand the importance of what they are experiencing; and thus we do not refer to the contact itself, but the message from the same..."
–Amaru, January 17, 1999

It all began on January 22, 1999, five days after receiving the aforementioned message. That day, journalists and technicians of the Dialogue program, on Channel 2 in Lima, experienced the sighting of their life.

Around midnight, while the van of the TV channel travelled on San Felipe Avenue in Lima, Jaime Vidal Torres, a professional camera operator, observed a strange object in the skies over the Peruvian capital. He had never seen anything like it, a "platform of lights" as he described the device again and again in interviews. It moved silently through the still night of Lima. Excited, the journalists chased the object and captured the experience on film.[1] In the video, you can see the clear pendulum motion of the object, swinging back and forth, above a crowd of witnesses who were amazed and had already begun spreading the word about the phenomenon.

Interestingly, it was the neighborhood where I lived.

However, I was not there at that time. I had gone to a camp in the Chilca desert, where about 130 people had gathered to evaluate and discuss 25 years of group contact with extraterrestrials. These experiences had started in this desolate coastal Peruvian landscape. They had continued to increase since the first message was received on January 22, 1974. It was on this same date that we had gathered in the wilderness, the main stage of close encounters with the "guides." It was therefore very suggestive that the wave of UFOs occurred in that location.

But the wave had just begun. The next day, at 11:10 am, a trader by the name of Percy Romero witnessed another UFO—at his house in Tumbes, in the far north of Peru. As described by Romero, it was an oval object of burnished metal. Thus, reports of sightings in Lima and in surrounding provinces became more numerous. All of Peru was being shaken by the appearance of these objects.

The main TV channels of the country, Channel 2, America Channel 4, and Channel 5 Pan-American, were involved in a real "UFO hunt." Many sightings were captured on film and were broadcast in prime time nationwide. As if this were not enough, the Peruvian Air Force (FAP) issued an official statement denying any political or military responsibility for

---

[1] The sighting was filmed on Barcelona Street, in the district of Pueblo Libre.

the transgression of Colombian airspace. Colombia, too, was reeling from appearances of "mysterious unidentified craft" thought to be from Peru.

The legacy of the IPRI

The UFO research group at *Instituto Peruano Relaciones Interplanetarias*[2] (IPRI), based in downtown Lima, is the largest and oldest in Latin America. IPRI closely followed this wave of UFO sightings, which involved various parts of the country, such as Arequipa and Cusco. There, strange lights, cloud trails and circular marks were left on the ground in the areas of Chincheros, Moquegua, Trujillo, Piura and Iquitos, among other cities. The wave of anomalies lasted until late March. On March 7, we conducted another field trip to the desert of Chilca, in order to check out the intense UFO activity reported there. To add to this detail, we were sure that the source of the object sighted in Lima was underwater installations located off the coast of Chilca, Puerto Viejo and Leon Dormido, and that these installations held extraterrestrials. In addition, the disturbing testimony of several fishermen, who claimed to have seen "luminous disks" on the beach of Las Salinas in Chilca during the wave of sightings, supported this information.

In the UFO circles of Lima it has been known, since the 1950s, that UFOs frequently appeared in the sea of Chilca. According to messages received in contact experiences, this was due to the existence of impermanent underwater installations, necessary because mother ships stay in the seabed, seasonally. Small scout ships, discs, or other objects of 20- to 30-meters in diameter would arise from the sea. These devices carried a crew of no more than seven passengers. The Chilca fishermen reported

---

[2]Peruvian Institute of Interplanetary Relations

the sighting of such objects minutes before they were seen and filmed in Lima.

We were not the only ones to find ourselves in Chilca on March 7. In the desert mountains to the east was a team of IPRI members. The team was led by its president, Don Carlos Paz Garcia Corrochano, a smart and intense character. Don Carlos was the pioneer of UFO research in America and Peru. He founded a research institute in 1955, well before the advent of Project Blue Book, the U.S. Air Force military project that sought to unravel the mystery of the unidentified. In the 1970s, Don Carlos's older sons, Carlos and Sixto Paz Wells, built on their father's work and initiated one of the most important collective experiences of Spanish contact.

On the night of March 7, as reported by those were who with him, Don Carlos suffered a fatal heart attack, apparently caused by over-excitement while observing one of the ships over Chilca.

His youngest daughter, the late Rose Marie Paz Wells who died in 2004, was my dear friend and an extraordinary researcher. Of her father she said, "My father died doing what he loved, investigating that which he loved so much, the mystery of UFOs."

The death of Don Carlos, in the middle of the UFO wave that the extraterrestrials had planned, left a powerful testimony for the dedication of a man who, until the end of his days, continued to watch the stars and try to understand their mysteries.

Our testimony on television

The wave of sightings was so clear and prolonged that various television stations profiled the subject from every angle in TV specials. As a result, representatives of our group were invited to every televised UFO program as well as interviews on radio, newspapers, and magazines. It was the first time I had an opportunity to share, with a broad audience, my contact experience and the message that the extraterrestrials had given us.

This was their plan, to blanket the airspace with their ships, knowing that the news media would cover the story and, therefore, contact us to discuss the observations. It is safe to say that after this UFO wave in Peru, and the intense dissemination we made as a result thereof, all kinds of institutions—from the Circle of Astronomy at the University of Lima, the National Police, Masonic lodges and endless mystical and philosophical groups—invited us to lecture to them. The mind-set of the Peruvian citizen against a possible extraterrestrial visitation opened up to the point of reflecting, in subsequent surveys, that more than 70% of Lima's citizens believed in UFOs and alien visitation.

As I mentioned previously, my constant media exposure placed my job as a medical representative at risk. I had always received the respect and support of my bosses in regard to the UFO issue, including time away from work to lecture out of the country. However, things began to change with the continued media exposure. Many doctors I dealt with called the laboratory where I worked to express their dismay with my involvement with the UFO phenomenon. The wave of 1999 sightings resulted in my being fired and this changed the course of my life

A high-ranking executive at the lab confronted me and said, "Mr. González, you have to decide whether you will be a representative of the laboratory or the extraterrestrials."

I have always tried to keep things separate. In fact I was quite efficient with my responsibilities at work where, paradoxically, I was held in high regard by my superiors who had no doubt that I could pursue my professional responsibilities as well as my UFO interests. My exposure to the news media began to alert my colleagues to my extraterrestrial experiences and it became something that bothered the laboratory managers. It was through a subsequent reduction of staff, where I was covertly included, that my career with that company came to an end.

I later learned that the final determination of my dismissal came from a foreign business manager who detested the subject of UFOs. It was that manager who possibly influenced my superiors and colleagues at the laboratory. However, although I didn't want to be unemployed, I felt at peace when I finally signed my letter of resignation. The marketing manager, who was given the job of handling my resignation, said casually from behind his mahogany desk, "Take it like this, perhaps your extraterrestrial friends want you to devote yourself full time to talk about them."

When I heard this, I immediately remembered many different contact experiences I had with the "guides," where they consulted me about whether I was willing to devote myself full time to spreading my testimony. Had the time come? But, what would happen to me? How was I going to live? Until then, my outreach activities in Peru and abroad were free. I'd had a good salary working as a health advisor and had certainly been able to cover my own expenses. What would happen now?

I have found that we function as participants in a larger design. The truth is that since I left that office building, where I punched my timecard every morning, my steps have continuously led me to various destinations around the world to share my testimony of contact. Without any effort on my part, invitations to lecture internationally and give interviews multiplied. I decided to accept this responsibility. I confess that it was difficult, at first, to exchange the security of a monthly salary for conferences and activities that were unforeseeable and which required I cover a number of my own costs. Almost

Contact From Planet Apu

without realizing it, I was becoming an international authority on the subject of UFOs, a "contactee" who gave lectures around the world.

Above: With my beloved friend Rosemary Paz Wells, interviewed by astronomer, Abraham Levi, on Channel 4, during the UFO wave of 1999. It was the airing of this program that precipitated my dismissal at work.

It was a major challenge to navigate the huge demand on my time and to live like this, but everything seemed to accommodate these changes, as if guided or protected by an invisible force. I was able to live quietly, although without making me rich as some supposed. Contrary to what some critics of the UFO phenomenon argue, one does not make a fortune talking about puzzles and mysteries. At least, not in my case.

I have visited more than fourteen countries a year and fifty different cities, lecturing about extraterrestrial contact. Since 1999, when I decided to spread my testimony full time, until today as I write these lines, I have not stopped traveling and sharing. In fact, today, my trips have increased greatly. I am at home just three or four months a year.

Eventually, I realized the importance of all that we are doing to promote a different view of contact with beings from other worlds. The evidence is only circumstantial, however. What is relevant is the message.

This pivotal change in my life came, as noted, as a direct result of the UFO wave of 1999. The sightings of that year also forced the Peruvian Air Force to create an office to investigate the UFO phenomenon. It was not by chance that I was a guest lecturer at a conference alongside other UFO scholars such as, the Italian-Peruvian researcher Giorgio Piacenza. It was Giorgio who would later play an important role in the programmed sighting that Michael E. Salla experienced with the Apunians at Mount Shasta. At this military conference in Lima, I met the Spanish journalist JJ Benitez, who was also in attendance.

It was after receiving, from the extraterrestrials, the announcement of the scheduled sighting that occurred over the skies of Peru that I was able I was able to arrange a second scheduled sighting with the guides. This time, the sighting would be for a small group in Chilca, as requested by journalists. Thus, Giorgio Piacenza and a reporter from Channel 2, Hugo Cogorno, accompanied me to the desert for the sighting, which occurred at 9:00 pm on a cold Saturday night, March 13. Hugo Cogorno, who later worked for the BBC, enthusiastically recalled the appearance of a light crossing the sky, observing it until it was lost in the mountains.

Sightings by appointment

The third time I had a scheduled sighting was with reporters in Argentina. Several luminous objects appeared in the cloudy sky of Cordoba, near Ongamira, eight kilometers from Capilla del Monte.

Another group in attendance, working with what was called the *Code* program hosted by journalist Rolando Graña, saw and recorded the experience with us. It was Thursday, May 5, 2005. This sighting recently came to light in a publication, though their treatment of the subject was unfortunate. The story appeared in a tabloid, generating a tremendous debate amongst various TV programs in Buenos Aires. One of the journalists who came with us, Hernán Di Lorenzi, apologized, claiming he gave the raw footage of the sighting to the producer (Endemol). Although there was a delay in getting the report on the air and despite it being a misrepresentation of the event, Rolando Graña, then news director of Channel 2 in Buenos Aires, recognized that these strange lights had appeared as we had predicted. He also acknowledged that we did not ask for money nor place conditions on the journalists for taking them to the location in Capilla del Monte.

The mocking way this sighting was presented in the tabloid, in spite of it happening as planned, hit me very hard. The *guides* had indeed performed their part by presenting themselves at the exact day and hour, and yet, the TV channel mocked those lights and our testimony. It was then that I decided to no longer invite journalists or researchers to any contact experience with us. I wondered why we were doing this, if it wasn't reported responsibly. What would be required for the sightings, and all that implied, to be taken seriously?

I'm not ashamed to say I was angry and disappointed. However, fate often has things in store we cannot foresee and, consequently, eight years later an event in Argentina, with Antarel of Apu, occurred that restored my hope.

Chapter 5

MOUNT SHASTA AND EXTRATERRESTRIAL BASES

The key place for everything that was yet to come, as it turns out, is a mysterious mountain in the United States. It is an ancient volcano, now asleep, that struck me from the first time I visited it in California. When I camped on its slopes, where a haunting pine forest rises, I realized that it would be very important in my life. It is no wonder I have visited it more than fifteen times and, after each of those experiences, have left feeling renewed. I felt one with the magical landscape, which had become a common scene of UFO sightings and stories of alleged lost civilizations. It is important to summarize what Shasta means, since I would return there to see Antarel physically and, from there, he would arrange new scheduled sightings. Shasta hides an extraterrestrial base of the Apunians.

The mountain of contact

In my book *Intraterrestrial*[1], I dedicated several pages to Mount Shasta and its relationship to an alleged underground brotherhood of teachers, a set of evolved beings who live inside the mountain and who, on occasion, have been spotted. Apparently, this matter, unconnected to the phenomenon of UFOs and closer to that of the esoteric, is one of the keys to understand what Shasta hides.

---

[1] Edition Luciérnaga, Grupo Planeta España, 2011.

Shasta is the second highest peak in the Cascade Range of volcanoes. It is over 14,000 feet high and its summit is blanketed by a white layer of snow much of the year. It is situated in northern California, fifty-five miles north of Redding and forty miles south of Yreka, in a beautiful nature reserve called, Mount Shasta Wilderness, which in turn belongs to the Shasta-Trinity National Forest. It is a six-hour journey by car from San Francisco to the town of Shasta, which is in the foothills of the mountain. Shasta is a mystical town that reminds me of Capilla del Monte at the foot of Cerro Uritorco, in Argentina.

But what does Shasta mean? Historians believe that "Shasta," which now is the name of the town and the mountain itself, is derived from different sources. Some believe it could come from the Russian word *Tshastal*, meaning "white" or "pure." Interestingly, the French term *chaste* also means "white." However, the root of the name is actually an indigenous word, *Ieka*, meaning "White Mountain." In each case, the meaning alludes to the symbolism of white, with its intrinsic message of purity and spirituality. In addition, Shasta is reportedly the name of an Indian tribe that lived near Yreka in the 1800s. It is quite likely that the Indians were named after the mountain. Regarding its history, we know that in 1817 a Spanish explorer, Narcisco Fray Duran, made the first sighting of the mountain, which he called Jesus Maria. But several years later, in 1841, the Wilkes Expedition renamed it, Shasty Peak, and published the first picture of the mountain. Today, everyone calls it Shasta and this name has been displayed on maps of the United States since 1850.

As I said, I have visited Shasta many times. I have spent many nights camping in the middle of its forests, especially in the area known as Sand Flat, which is chosen by the Native Americans for ceremonies and rituals. I can attest that UFO sightings are frequently reported here, as well as the appearance of very bright silhouettes—humanoid figures that suddenly appear in the middle of nowhere and then simply vanish.

These "projections" are a demonstration of the alleged intraterrestrial brotherhood that lives inside the mountain. All this, as expected, has sparked much esoteric discussion. Were UFO reports connected with those from the underworld? Are these *white* men immaterial beings? Or is it indeed a race of intraterrestrial spacemen? It is also said that in the nineteenth century, these creatures bought local goods and paid with golden nuggets. There are a thousand and one stories that are all difficult to prove. Whatever the case, the phenomena of Shasta is, in essence, real as are the UFO sightings and glares of light on the mountain. More than a few suggest that the power of Shasta comes from its center, or terrestrial energy that has been locked away since ancient times. Some claim to see flashes near its summit. However, although it is considered a dormant volcano, perhaps its crater is producing a small plume of smoke. What is in there?

Intraterrestrial city? Apunian base?

In April 1972, James Hadouk, and Irving and William Lescer Schoner, students of geology at the University of Berkeley (California) climbed to the top of the mountain and found that the crater showed no sign of activity. That is, at that time, there were no reports of smoke plumes or earthquakes to suspect an awakening of the volcano. But, the adventure of the young college men did not end there. While resting at the crater after the research journey, shortly before descending the mountain, the young men watched, through binoculars, five tall white men, with abundant wavy hair, walking and then suddenly disappear behind a boulder at the foot of the dormant volcano. Who were these men in white? The geology students were impressed and told their story upon their return, which generated skepticism.

To all this, it is notable to consider the statements of Professor Edgar Lucin Larkin, former director of the Mount Lowe Observatory in Southern California. While using a powerful telescope, he distinguished a shining dome at the top of the mountain, surrounded by buildings. For the balance of his life, the astronomer defended what he saw on Shasta, publishing two articles in the *San Francisco Examiner*. Many, however, find the existence of Larkin's building impossible, for the mountain has been thoroughly covered by more than one climber. It has also been officially mapped and photographed by the Air Force with no findings of anything unusual. Notwithstanding this, the experience of Larkin coincides with that of many other witnesses. They saw something that perhaps *can* be explained.

In the esoteric world, it is said that multiple planes and dimensions exist. In fact, today it is studied by quantum physics. But it is one thing is to talk about particles and waves, and quite another to speak of entities and cities of energy. Were the buildings that Professor Lucin Larkin saw on the Shasta summit a "holographic projection" of the intraterrestrial city alleged to be hidden there?

According to the Hopi Indians, Shasta hides a secret. They say that the survivors of the sinking world Kasskara, submerged in the Pacific Ocean about 12,000 years ago, were brought to America in "flying shields" and "Birds of Fire" by cosmic gods called, Kachinas, a name that can be translated as "venerable, judge, and wise." This finding is surprising since the Hopi Indian Reservation is currently settled in Arizona, far from Shasta, and is considered to be one of the places where the survivors "landed" in birds of fire. Josef F. Blumrich, a NASA engineer who reconstructed a model of the ship, saw this description in the biblical texts of the prophet Ezekiel. Aware of the Hopi legends, the American scientist collected, directly from the Hopi, White Bear, fifty hours of recorded conversations. When one is faced with these fascinating stories, one cannot avoid the obligatory question: Who were the Kachinas? Why do the Hopi say that these gods came from the Pleiades? Did an extraterrestrial civilization help the inhabitants of Kasskara in their exodus to Shasta? Was all of this part of the "Cosmic Plan" mentioned in previous pages of this book?

According to Blumrich, the Kachinas were physical beings who needed ships to transport them. They are not the ethereal figures of "gods," but cosmonauts.

The survivors of Kasskara or "Mu," its esoteric name, are often confused with those from Lemuria in the Indian Ocean. Aided by beings from the Pleiades, they took refuge in the bowels of the White Mountain to deposit important files and knowledge of their civilization. According to this, Shasta is a vast underground vault with ancient relics of lost files and cultures.

In our communication with extraterrestrials, they confirmed to us the extraordinary Hopi history, and added that, in the area where the dormant volcano rises, there is an important base that brings together different civilizations from other worlds. Among them, an Apunian scientific laboratory. This could explain why Antarel chose Mount Shasta for the scheduled sightings and physical contact.

According to Antarel, the Apunians have different bases on our world, most of them in the Andes. Among those that we are able to reveal, the most active today include:

Mount Shasta, United States
Mount Perdido, the Pyrenees, Spain

Siberia, Russia
Annapurna Region, Nepal
Tepoztlán, México
Huascarán National Park, Perú
Andes of Huánuco y Pasco Hill, Perú
Ausangate, Cusco, Perú
Submarine Base, off the coast of Chilca, Perú
Green Lagoon (Licancabur), Bolivia
Window Mountain Range, Argentina
Talampaya, Argentina
Somuncura, Argentina
Submarine base facing the islands of Chiloe, Chile

In addition, Antarel noted that they have facilities in Antarctica. According to him, most of these bases are not permanent structures but laboratory-ships, located on sites of scientific interest or "nodes" of power in our world. Some of these bases are only entry and exit portals to extra-dimensional levels, as in the case of the Window Mountain range, Argentina. Others are larger installations, such as the one located in the Huascarán in Yungay, in the Peruvian Andes. This will be discussed later.

The Apunians can physically manifest anywhere they desire, even in the very room where a witness is located. They are not limited to direct contact with humans occurring only near the location of their bases. There are protocols of contact. One protocol is that if the witness answers their invitation and goes by choice to a preset "contact zone," the extraterrestrial is able to provide more information.

There are the "rules" of those cosmic civilizations that seek to interfere as little as possible in human life. They try to help, but within those limitations of action. It is necessary to consider what can be done, and yet a very different thing to consider what should be done according to our values and ethical behavior as a species in human learning. Shasta, then, was the chosen setting.

It was there that I would reencounter Antarel.

Contact From Planet Apu

Chapter 6

INSIDE A SPACESHIP

On January 22, 2010, I was in a contact camp in Paraguay. The place where we met the extraterrestrial guides was the Ybytiruzú Mountains, about 11 miles east of the city of Villarrica.

While meditating in front of the symbols of the stonewall of Ita, a place that reminds me of the Pusharo rock in the jungles of Manu in Peru, I received a message from Antarel, inviting me to a new physical encounter. According to the brief communication of the extraterrestrial Apunian, this would take place on August 8, in the desert of Chilca.

I should mention here that I have been living in Buenos Aires since 2002, and have been traveling from Argentina, throughout the world, spreading the message of the contact experience. Traveling back to Peru that August, I was filled with many emotions, as I prepared to encounter Antarel in Chilca. I was excited to share the message from Antarel with Francisco Camacho, a dear friend and associate of the contact groups of Asuncion. I met with Francisco and requested a sighting of corroboration with the extraterrestrials. If the invitation was genuine, *they* had to show up. And so they did at the appointed time. We witnessed, at that exact moment, the appearance of a bright object above a pyramidal hill.

That sighting made me take the invitation I had received very seriously. So, I assumed that I should prepare for the "date."

Shortly after my trip to Paraguay, I contacted several friends, all active participants in these contact experiences. My intention was to form a sympathetic team of that could accompany me to Peru to attend the Chilca desert. Thus, the group was formed with Ruben Astacio of Dominican Republic, Isabel Cabral of Honduras, Cuckie and Elard Pastor of Lima, Raymundo Collazo and Ricardo Zapata of the United States and Argentina.

The experiences can be postponed

On August 8, 2010, we reached the desert of Chilca, located an hour and a half drive from the city of Lima. As always, the desert greeted us with deafening silence. Amid this haunting, but beautiful place, we assembled our tents and prepared for the experience. As night fell, we received new communications and found the *guides* to be timely, through several sightings. It was a sign that the contact would occur. But, when the time came for the experience, I felt I could not continue. I was not ready.

I realized that a close and direct experience with the extraterrestrials went beyond the anecdotal phenomenon. I was aware that physical contact with them would involve the specific needs of their agenda and would require notes and information of all kinds and, consequently, the taking on of certain tasks. Troubled by misgivings about being emotionally ready for another contact that would generate additional tasks, I decided not to face this new experience of physical contact. I realized, at that moment in Chilca, that I was not ready emotionally to take on any task—no new orders, no additional responsibilities, nothing.

Earlier, in February 2010, having received an invitation for contact in Paraguay, I had had to face a tough personal situation that weighed heavily on my mind. Although it was one of those trials of life that makes one grow, it was still hard to assimilate. I knew the *brothers* had planned the entire cosmos to the millimeter, but I could not get over the situation I had experienced. I know that they always trusted me, and for that reason kept the current invitation open. However, in the end, my mood betrayed me and I dared not meet them in Chilca. We left Peru empty handed.

Through a new communication with them, I said I would wait until I felt ready.

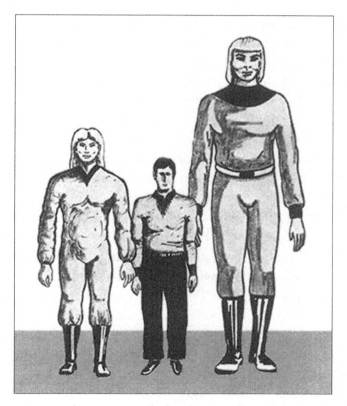

Above: A drawing that compares the height of an alien colony on Ganymede, Orion beings on the mysterious moon of Jupiter, that of a human being, and finally an Apunian, who stands out with his height. Drawing from the book UFOs, SOS Mankind, JJ Benitez, Editorial Plaza & Janes, Barcelona, 1975.

As I said earlier, I had seen Antarel in other experiences. One of the most dramatic occurred in the same Peruvian desert, on February 24, 2001. On that occasion, they allowed me, for the first time, to climb inside a space ship. This was possible thanks to a beam of light that can absorb a person upward without causing harm. Once onboard, I was led into a large round room, well lit by a bright white light that penetrated everything. In that experience, Antarel and another extraterrestrial, humanoid in appearance, gave me lots of information about them and listed many events that would eventually occur, such as the unfortunate attack on the Twin Towers in New York, which happened seven months after this contact. It was important to share this experience with the news media in the United States before the September 11 incidents. For the extraterrestrials, that would be a key event that would change the rules worldwide. Again, they would be right.

In that contact of 2001, Antarel had briefly spoken of Apu, confirming that his home world had been destroyed and the Apunians, as a result, became space travelers in time, settlers on other planets where they established new homes. Their main colony settled on a world of Alpha Centauri. This new Apu would have come to Earth after having established transit colonies in our Solar System. Something that intrigued me about that conversation with Antarel was my being asked to investigate the Longshot Project. I was not aware it existed until I heard the words spoken by the giant Apunian. I kept this information from the original report and my previous books because, I didn't really understand the implications of it and felt unprepared to discuss it with people.

The project is a design of an interstellar unmanned spacecraft scheduled to travel to Alpha Centauri. The report is available on the internet today. That ship is to be driven by nuclear pulse propulsion in order to reach that sector of space involving Antarel's civilization. Developed by the US Naval Academy and NASA, Longshot was designed to be built in the much larger Space Station, Alpha, the forerunner of the current International Space Station.

Investigating all this in 2001, I had the feeling that Antarel revealed something, something that could change our perception of them, though I wasn't exactly sure what it was.

So, as I say, I put in "quarantine" what the Apunian had awakened in me to give me this clue.

What exactly am I attempting to convey in this new physical contact?

After the failed 2010 meeting in Chilca, I returned from my travels. I was focused on what had taken place until new communications reminded me that Antarel's invitation to contact was still open and that I needed to prepare for it.

Invitation to a dormant volcano

It happened exactly a year after the trip to Peru. Mount Shasta, in August 2011, was one of the most important events to verify that physical contact could occur on a programmed basis. That year, I was on this beautiful mountain in California when Antarel again began to send telepathic messages that I must prepare for contact.

Then, on February 26, 2012, finding myself in Tepoztlan, Mexico, the guides sent me a visual and auditory telepathic message, once again inviting me to physical contact.

"I reiterate the invitation for you to come back with us. If it was not important, we would have not asked you. You are prepared."
–Oxalc

On July 18, in Buenos Aires, the extraterrestrials again invited me to contact with these words, *"In August, the conditions* will be appropriate to act on our earlier invitation. We reiterate, it will be at the foot of the dormant volcano." –Antarel

In early August I was at Sajama, the volcano in Bolivia, attending to tasks from the extraterrestrials in order to prepare myself at this very important center of power. I was accompanied to Sajama by a group of dear friends. It was here that I had an extraordinary experience that demonstrated the abilities of the cosmic brothers. On the night of August 6, at the foot of Sajama in the Bolivian Andes and under the lights of the ships that were stationed in the area, we experienced a series of flashes. A strange force fell on me and I raised 6 to 8 inches off the ground. Sol, my partner, was at my side and witnessed this event.

That night, still shaken by what had happened, Antarel explained the strange occurrence in a visual and auditory telepathic message.

"We gave you a test, raising you from the ground. It is to remind you to take future invitations with responsibility and consciousness. The conditions are set for a direct encounter with us this August." –Antarel

The coordinates of the contact were given the next day after I photographed an anomalous object approaching Sajama, an event that Ruben Astacio, from the Domicanan Republic also captured with his camera. We began to understand the connection immediately, which allowed us to receive the message that the extraterrestrials confirmed Mount Shasta as the contact site. They also confirmed the exact date: Sunday, August 26 of that same year, 2012. This was to happen very shortly!

I had scheduled in Shasta, as every year, my annual meditation retreat. It so happened that this was taking place on the same date as the meditation. How was I to have physical contact during this activity? I had to trust and also be cautious.

In order to avoid expectations that could affect the experience, I did not publicly disclose the contact invitation. However, I must disclose that I communicated privately with different groups in Spain, the USA, Mexico, El Salvador, Honduras, Dominican Republic, Argentina, Peru, Chile, Paraguay, Bolivia, among others, requesting their support from a distance.

This time the experience was different from that of 2010. I understood the importance of the invitation and, for two years, had been mentally preparing for what I would experience.

The preparation

When my plane arrived in the United States, I could not hide my nervousness and excitement. *"I will physically see Antarel again,"* I reflected. My companion, Sol, kept me grounded and supported me as I waited for what seemed to be forever.

At the foot of Mount Shasta, fifty-five people gathered from various countries, mostly residents of the United States and Mexico. Since I had come to the mountain with an advance team, on Friday night, August 24, the extraterrestrials began to show themselves.

The first thing I did was to walk to Sand Flat, where we would set up camp. Sol came with me.

Standing there, I tried to communicate with *them*. I just wanted to know they were there. A bright orange-colored object appeared in the sky and then disappeared into the clear night, against a backdrop of the crescent moon. Excited, we requested the extraterrestrials to return to verify their presence, and thus, an unmanned probe appeared, a sort of "electronic eye" or

Canepla, as we call it in our contact circles. It moved with some speed, at a very low altitude, almost touching the tops of the pines. It was extraordinary.

When we returned to the advance team, Carlos Federico of Mexico and Mary Fajardo of Colombia warned me that there had been some strange flashes of energy in the sky. I also saw flashes similar to those witnessed at other gatherings in Chilca. They were not flares from Iridium satellites. These satellites can cause confusion in the UFO field and have a peculiar form, with three flat, polished antennas angled at 120 degrees of separation. Occasionally, one of these antennas reflects sunlight directly toward Earth, creating a false bright star for a few seconds. The phenomenon reaches a brightness magnitude of about -8 (but rarely reaches -9.5). [Editor's note: On this astronomer's scale, smaller numbers represent brighter objects, so a magnitude of -8 is about twenty times brighter than Venus.] Some flares are so bright that they can be seen even in daylight, but are more impressive at night. However, apparently on Shasta that night, it was something else and it was behaving intelligently.

As in Sajama, where I was elevated off the ground, I felt that there was, above us, a stationary spaceship. Without much thought, I took a digital camera that I had at that time, which had a 42x optical zoom, and snapped a photograph, catching a pulsating light moving and changing from white to blue. I took several pictures, making sure the camera was operating properly. In the pictures you can see the movement of the object, as if it were drawing symbols against the fixed stars in the background as a reference to its movement.

Thus, we were greeted by the mountain.

Later, *they* reappeared and, with this new sighting, we were able to interact with one of their space ships, which was very high at its zenith. It lit up with power whenever we pointed our halogen flashlight in their direction. It was very beautiful.

Although I knew I could not, I really wished I could include the large group that was beginning to gather on Shasta. I found it difficult, as they were very interested and wanted to witness the approach of our elder brothers. However, I had to be responsible and not risk this new opportunity to meet with Antarel.

Following this protocol, I related the sighting only to a small group: Raul Dominguez and his wife, Lorraine, both of San Francisco; Alma Reyes, Suyapa Reyes and Luis Ochoa from Napa Valley; and Mary Fajardo and Carlos Federico, who lived in San Francisco. Sol and I completed the group. However later, due to wonderful synchronicities, four more people joined us.

I finished my retreat on August 26 at noon, having experienced some very special moments during meditation. As I said, Shasta is compelling. I love the pine forest and the silhouette of this silent mountain, which rises above the huge trees as a supernatural guardian. As always, in our camps, some personal experiences occurred within the forest that spoke to us and taught us. It is a forest that initiates you into the truth, as if it were a powerful shaman. Many in the camp saw the light phenomena during their walks, as well as orbs and energies of all kinds.

On the night of the 25th I had received a telepathic message from Antarel, which was accompanied by an invitation to a new sighting. My old extraterrestrial friend confirmed to me that on Sunday, August 26 at 9:00 pm, they would show themselves and, after that, I would meet them in a forest clearing, which he showed me telepathically. Without delay, I shared this with the group and they were aware of the invitation. We had to stay focused on what was coming.

At noon on August 26, we closed the seminar by connecting, in meditation, two volcanoes, Sajama and Shasta, two centers of power from which we sent light to everyone. By this, I do not mean that world peace will be achieved only by meditating for the planet. Peace is an inner state and begins with a knowledge of energy as it has been transmitted to us by the extraterrestrials. We practice exercises to stimulate the human ability to co-create reality. I clarify this because our experiences have nothing to do with a manipulation of extraterrestrial beings to open portals to the darkside. We avoid any generalizations about the universe, which might be synonymous with fear and ignorance. Over many years, we have carried out these meetings with this type of meditation and obtained positive results for all who attend. It would be incorrect to imply otherwise.

It was amazing that during our work at Shasta, an intense wind sometimes appeared, swirling around us. Many of us feel that the wind of Shasta was driven by something invisible. It was not a natural wind. Francisco Huerta of Mexico did note that a cloud had formed over the mountain on one occasion. The strange thing is that this cloud was there for only one hour, hanging in the clear blue sky. It then disappeared without a trace. It was not steam or ash from a dormant volcano. Shasta is world-renowned for this phenomenon, which seems to indicate an energy specific to this place. Shasta scholars claim that the mountain holds the world record for the formation of lenticular clouds.

After all of that, we left the camp and went up the mountain path along the route to the viewpoint, just ten minutes away by car. The landscape viewed from this place is extraordinary. There, we had a new sighting in broad daylight. It was brief, but very close up. The approach and shape of this craft reminded me of the old UFO photographs captured by Eduard "Billy" Meier in Switzerland. Sol, Aleyda Galeano (Colombia), and George Melendez (El Salvador), saw a kind of metallic, flat, white disk, which reflected sunlight. Excited, we tried to film and photograph it, but it was impossible. It did not appear in the camera! We saw it, but literally, it did not appear in the camera as we looked through the viewer. However, I kept shooting. All that it is seen in the video is the blue sky, as if the object had been made invisible to our technology. However, we clearly saw it, if only for a few moments.

The disc vanished from the sky in an instant.

I felt that the extraterrestrials had done this as a demonstration, and knew, in that moment, that contact was most certainly going to happen.

Frequently, I am asked how one can prepare to live this kind of experience. I usually mention that, if it is true, there are all kinds of meditation techniques that help you relax and raise your personal frequency in order to face a close encounter with beings wielding a very high vibratory rate. It is the extraterrestrials who ultimately decide who, how, and under what circumstances to show themselves. It would be childish to assume that people who experience contact are "chosen." I do not feel like that. I do not live like that. I understand that this happens, as I explained, by the needs of a "program," which has its objectives and tasks. I think some contact witnesses, as in my humble case, have always been part of the program. The main preparation was becoming mentally balanced: focusing my thoughts on contact and understanding my own perception about the extraterrestrials and my concern for how I would live my life. What people would think once they knew my testimony, and identifying the "ghosts" I had to leave behind. It was not easy. It wasn't only through meditation, but also self-observation that I managed to better understand my ghosts. In learning by trial and error, through daily contact with these beings, and through my outreach around the world, I began to understand how this all works. It is as simple as ceasing to see them as "extraterrestrials," who come in spaceships carrying cosmic stories, and, instead, seeing them as one of us. It was like rediscovering old family.

Understanding things in this way would move us away from any sectarian stance, a very dangerous thing I have seen germinating in different contact groups. This stance develops when analysis and common sense are lost, and when one depends on a leader or the extraterrestrials themselves. Without exaggerating, I have sometimes seen that a kind of cult is established which creates dogma that cannot be questioned. I do not agree with this sectarian approach and, for that reason, have decided to stay away from it and remain independent in what I do. It is not my desire to form "groups" or gain "followers," but only to share my testimony and message. My path is free and, therefore, I encourage freedom.

I have also seen how some people have become tremendously confused by these experiences, believing they are now special beings, bearers of a mission that no one else can understand. Some have even taken or appropriated the name of extraterrestrials and then dressed in white and surrounded themselves by followers, proclaiming themselves to be messengers from other dimensions. It has even happened with some who are connected to Antarel. I think it is a dangerous delusion to present oneself with the name of a being from another world.[1]

Despite my use of the term "extraterrestrial" throughout this book to facilitate the understanding of readers who are new to the topic, my perception of them is quite different. They are

---

[1] In 2013, an individual from Cordoba, Argentina began to appear in public using the name "Antarel Elohim." Of course, our experience of contact with the extraterrestrials of Apu has nothing to do with the messianic delirium. Antarel is not an "angel" or "dimensional energy," but a solid, biological being who has been seen by multiple witnesses. We condemn such situations that only confuse the real message of Contact.

simply older brothers of the cosmos! They are beings of older races. They are from older civilizations and have had different experiences. They are not better, but simply at a further stage in the evolutionary process. Many things await the human race, including communication with ethical and respectful civilizations.

Reunion with Antarel

Once most of the participants left my Shasta retreat, a small group of us went back to Sand Flat at about 7:00 pm. We found that the place was changed. One of our party, Lucia, felt a penetrating energy and I felt it was due to the meditation work of the entire group over the past few days. I also had the sensation that the mountain was glowing.

At Sand Flat, we found Francisco Huerta and Alberto Arreola, Maria Pascuala (El Salvador), and Emilio Salazar (Mexico). They had felt the need to delay their departure from Shasta, completely unaware of my contact invitation, although "Pascuala," as we affectionately call her, knew contact was going to occur that night, and, therefore, wanted to stay a little longer. As such, the group consisted of thirteen people.

At that time, I reminded all of them what could happen. 9:00 pm was the appointment for physical contact. We had to be together and not get nervous before any demonstration could occur. We were now alone, high on the mountain, and the presence that I felt there was shocking. Everything was different.

We all agreed to meditate and practice energy-raising methods through the use of mantras. We were to begin at 8:00 pm. However, the contact would occur no matter what we did, because it was prearranged. However, over the years we had learned that it is important to remain connected as a refined, heterogeneous group in order to achieve as high a vibration as possible. We did it without difficulty. The group was very united, focused and quiet. Raul Dominguez led the preparation work. During this, I received the following telepathic message through automatic writing:

Yes, we are near.

You have done important work on the mountain. You connected an energy network that linked the centers of power (referring to Sajama and Shasta).

We will approach you, brother. Watch for our demonstration. It will be between 9:00 and 9:30 pm. With the signal, you will go to the place we previously indicated, in the clearing in the woods.

We will be there. It depends on you.

With love,
Antarel

After the message, I closed my notebook and continued working with the group. I looked at my watch. It was 8:50 pm, 10-minutes away from the time contact was to begin.

I was very excited, just as with my first contacts in the Chilca desert. As if it were a ritual, we went over my history, such as the sightings when I was a child, the UFO sighting from 1998 when I was fired from work, all of it.

I perceived that Antarel and other guides were near me. I visualized their approach. I had an indescribable feeling at the thought of seeing them again, but I was also nervous. Everything was very intense, and many old experiences and memories assailed me at that moment. It was as if I was living it all over again.

I tried to reassure myself and I think I greatly succeeded.

I looked at my watch: 8:59 pm. I did not take my eyes off of it.

I thought to myself, will they be punctual this time? The entire group knew the time of the appointment. I had announced it just like that. I wondered, if they are not on time, how would it affect the group? How would it affect me? In the message, I had been told they were going to be there, and now it was up to me. I thought, do you want to live this again? With all its meaning? Are you really sure?

One minute seemed to be a very long time, not unlike other contact moments I had lived through, but I decided and my answer was yes.

As soon as my watch showed 9:00 pm, I got up slowly, turned my eyes toward the sky, and there they were.

In a very clear sky, the powerful moon was as bright as day, allowing only a few stars to be seen, and generating moon shadows of us on the ground. A beautiful, bright object—an orange-yellow, an intense, great color—came flying low, moving slowly and silently, surrounding the area where the group was. It was an indisputable sighting.

Looking at the object, overwhelmed by joy, my colleagues said, "It is 9:00 pm!" While in the midst of the hubbub, they had looked at their watches.

Here was the sign that *they* had fully complied.

Without much thought, I stood up and said goodbye to the group, starting toward the clearing in the forest we had agreed on before.

At first, the group was so enthusiastic about the appearance that they all got up from the meditation and talked excitedly among themselves, trying to comprehend this appearance.

Despite the clarity of the sighting, no one could fully understand the implications

Suyapa Reyes suggested that they provide support while I made contact. The group returned to the practice of meditation and did so with such a force and intensity that I could feel it during my walk.

As I approached the place where I had seen the extraterrestrials during my previous personal experience, I heard, in the distance, the mantras of the group, and was keenly aware of the many friendly people who were here in support of this invitation. I did not feel alone at any time. But, nevertheless, when I got to the place where the experience was going to occur, I had to breathe deeply, so intense was the presence of *them* in the forest. I became a little nervous. Although I had seen them before in other physical encounters, the energy that is present is overwhelming. Moreover, the fact of knowing that I would board one of their ships filled me with feelings that were indescribable.

A second luminous ship appeared in the sky above the forest. It flew over me and seemed to head towards the group.

Something pulled me out of my concentration. Something unexpected. I heard some children playing nearby, I could hear them laughing. I thought, there are no other people camping here.

The voices came from the clearing in the direction I was headed. I was puzzled. I saw a group of five or six children, including one who was a very young blonde little girl, playing and hanging around the area. Most of them were about seven years old and appeared to be American children.

In that moment, I forgot about the contact.

I wondered where are their parents? What is going on?

I walked towards them mesmerized. It did not seem to disturb them that I was there. They ran toward me, holding hands, and formed a circle around me. As they began to walk around in a circle, with me in the middle, a strong flash, like a very bright white glow, came from everywhere and forced me to close my eyes. I felt a powerful force rip me upward, just as had happened to me in 2001, in Chilca.

Suddenly, I found myself standing in a large circular room. Because of the flash, it took time for my eyes to adjust. I could only make out the circular form of the chamber, where a marked silence reigned. In front of me, I began to see the silhouette of two people.

It was completely quiet inside and I tried to assess the situation. When my eyes adjusted to the living area, I noticed that it was about eighty feet in diameter, and a large oval door opened in the circular wall. There I saw two *guides* whom I knew well, Anitac and Antarel, standing on either side of the door. Anitac was to my left, smiling, holding in her hand a black metal cube that reminded me of an object I had seen before in the Chilca contact. Anitac was wearing a one-piece silver suit, her hands and face uncovered. She is a woman, appearing to be in her 40s, very light blond hair, about 5'6". This is not the case with Antarel, a giant Apunian, who was to my right and closer to me. He is about 9 feet tall. Their bodies are perfect, but not due to any special training. Genetically, they are "perfect" human beings, but more stylized. To see that they have a nose, mouth and hair, makes me think that their home worlds are not so different from ours. Antarel also had a form-fitting metallic suit similar to Anitac's. His long, straight, blond-gray hair was so bright that it appeared artificial. His honey colored eyes, as human as ours, radiated something familiar. Something that made me feel a part of them.

"Welcome back," Antarel told me, telepathically, as I smiled.

"You created an illusion of children," I told them.

"Remember that we are mental doctors," Antarel responded. "We can generate very real holograms for you. We did it so that you would relax before bringing you aboard."

"How do I know that I am not now in a hologram?" I replied, although I knew that I was physically there with them.

Antarel, still smiling and with an expression of tenderness, came towards me, causing my body to shudder. He put his left hand on my chest, pressing his giant index and middle fingers into my chest. While looking into my eyes, he said, out loud, in perfect Spanish, "Richard, we are always with you. I am your friend, your brother."

I do not know how to convey this. It was one of the most intense moments of the entire experience. I had not previously heard them speak. I knew they could learn our languages, but they always used telepathic communication in these encounters.

Hearing him speak in my language and call me by my human name, while touching my chest, was one of the most wonderful gifts I have ever had in my life.

Ricardo González

Above: Vitko Novi.

Below: From Easter Island to Patagonia, we have had evidence of the Apunian ships, spherical objects, discoid, "boomerang" or tubular.

Contact From Planet Apu

Above: The displacement of an Apunian spaceship during a scheduled contact in Talampaya, Argentina, in January 2015. Photo by Cristian Belluco.

Above: Dr. Michael E. Salla, one of the fathers of Exopolitics.

Below: A screenshot of one of the UFOs that appeared during the scheduled contact that Salla participated in on Mount Shasta (2013).

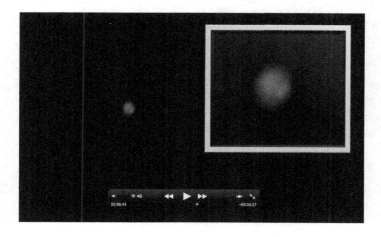

Contact From Planet Apu

Above: The author at Sand Flat, at the foot of Mount Shasta.
Below: One of the contact meetings and meditation.

Ricardo González

Above: Ricardo González and Paola Harris, after successful contact on Mount Shasta (2014).

Below: A screenshot from one of the videos taken of the ships, filmed with night vision equipment.

Contact From Planet Apu

Above: Observatory La Silla in the Atacama region in Chile. From there, a planet near the star Alpha Centauri B in the Alpha Centauri star system was discovered.

Below: The recreation of an astronomical discovery. Do other worlds with viable living conditions exist in this sector of space? Are our scientists looking for Apu?

Ricardo González

Above: The famous Russian cosmonaut Alexei Leonov, in recent statements, suggested that future astronauts must be children.

Below: A representation of NASA's Warp Drive, which theoretically could travel to Alpha Centauri in just two weeks, thanks to the impulse curvature of space-time.

Contact From Planet Apu

Above: A picture of Huascarán from Christ the Redeemer, which marks the location of the buried city of Campo Santo in Yungay. In that snow-capped, Andean mountain in Peru, the main base of the Apunians would be found.

Below: Taking a flight from Lima to that magical region of Ancash (April 2015).

Ricardo González

Above: The expeditionary group in Ancash at the home of Don Tobias Sarmiento, former employee of the Huallanca Hydropower Plant (where Kapetanovic's contact happened in 1960).

Below: The author with Sarmiento, checking his files on Apunians.

Above: The author at a dam in Callejón de Huaylas (the Alley of Huaylas), Ancash.

Below: Llanganuco, Yungay.

Above: The author in Ichic Puna, Yungay.
Below: Detail of the stone where contact happened on April 12, 2015.

Above: Drawing of Antarel by the Argentine artist Ramiro Rossi.

Chapter 7

INTERVIEW WITH AN APUNIAN

"*You are physically here,*" Antarel continued, but telepathically, while he slowly withdrew his fingers from my chest. "*It was important that this experience unfold in this manner. We have connected with you since you were a child, and we guided you to contact groups, when you were a boy as part of a training plan. Now you are a man and we are still with you. This has been the same process for many of you.*"

What the Apunian said was true, and it was amazing to see that this extraterrestrial being, whom I had originally met many years before in Chilca, still looked like a young man, about 35 years of age in appearance, though they can actually live thousands of our years. Now I looked older than him.

I would have loved to photograph Antarel, but that evidence is not allowed for several reasons. When I asked them why, they cited three crucial points: First of all, the extraterrestrial organization to which the Confederacy belongs does not allow them to give "direct evidence." That is their protocol with our human society.

The second reason is that some of them can adapt or mutate to look like us. They do not want to be detected. A photograph is not a drawing, it captures their real image and this might compromise them. Those extraterrestrials that have infiltrated our world have penetrated our military bases, scientific laboratories, and facilities of all kinds. But they have not done it because they are collaborating with any government or specific military personnel, but because they try to monitor our activities and warn us, as far as possible, so that we do not hurt ourselves. The third reason they do not give us direct evidence is because it could endanger them.

To see Antarel's eyes was like looking at the universe through a man of the stars. As I say, the Apunian had not aged, at least not in relation to my biological rhythm. He looked just the same as in the first contact. This made me feel that our human life is very, very short.

"*Man's life on Earth is just an instant, brother,*" he said to me. "*We have another perception of time and life. Thus, we understand your doubts, questions and requirements. We would like to explain many things to you, but everything must be given in small doses and timed so that you may assimilate it in the best way.*"

"Why am I in one of your ships again?" I said to him aloud. "And wasn't there an easier, a different way, perhaps through the doors that you usually open?" referring to why I was there in their craft once again. You can see I was more relaxed after Antarel spoke to me in Spanish.

This was no longer a dialogue between a witness and an extraterrestrial being that I had seen before. Antarel created an environment of confidence and naturalness, placing me at ease, despite the extraordinary experience this was for me.

"*You had to be physically here with us,*" he told me slowly and reassuringly.

"*Aren't the* Xendras, *or dimensional portals, that you usually open physical?*" I mentally asked the question, utilizing the standard method of telepathic contact.

"*We know that you have already been reflecting upon it. There are different doors, creases and experiences, and all of them happen at different levels in accordance with what we program, as well as, proper preparation of the witnesses. Nevertheless, even through those dimensional doors allow us or you to physically transport, the energy that moves is subtler, it utilizes and connects other types of forces. It is, in other words, a parallel, holographic reality. So, in some contact experiences they turn out to be light and perceive everything differently, although they are physically there."*

"I understand..."

"The Xendras were established from the beginning of the contact as the main tool to have close encounters with you," he continued. "It is a less traumatic way for you to meet and train with us in other inter-dimensional realities that will embrace the Earth in a near future. The physical contacts that require a closer relationship with us are individual ones. In some instances, we have tried encounters with groups of people, but we did not have great success."

"Why do they have to be individual ones? Why do you find the group encounters difficult to handle?"

"Because this is how it has been stipulated in our protocol of direct non-intervention. Our ethical behavior with you involves a profound respect for human learning, and that process on Earth does not allow us to affect groups of witnesses in physical collective encounters, if they are not completely aligned. That is to say, it does not depend only on us and our conduct, but also on your group preparation. Greater human physical interaction is on our agenda, but the time has not come yet. Inter-dimensional experiences that do not completely involve the physical plane on which humans base their perception, it turns out, is a simpler way to connect several witnesses at a time. That way we do not affect humans in their everyday life. The Xendras provide a coping mechanism for the human brain that is similar to the dynamics of dreams. That way you (humans) can overall assimilate the experience better. In accordance with the content we want to transmit, the Xendra becomes the vehicle for the programmed experience that we choose."

"Was this the reason the contact had to be experienced here, and in this way?"

"If we had taken you to Celia (an orbital base behind the Moon, which I became aware of during an experience in 2001) or into the Cave de los Tayos (the door to the underworld in Ecuador, which I visited in 2002) through a Xendra, your perception would not have been the same. It is always true that the most important element of a contact experience will be the message or the content of the experience and not the phenomenon that surrounds it; but certain things are understood differently when the contact is experienced in each of its stages. For your work with the programmed contact, it was necessary for you to experience it materially. We also determined that you could mentally withstand all this."

Antarel, on other occasions, had already stressed this point, the importance of a witness's mental plasticity and the ability of a witness to adapt to a disturbing experience, that being contact with an extraterrestrial. In psychology and modern neuroscience, this condition is called resilience, which is the ability of an individual to overcome adverse situations or emotional stress. When an individual or group is capable of overcoming this type of stress, they are said to have adequate resilience, and this stress may even fortify the individual or group after an intense experience. The extraterrestrials meticulously study a witness before contact to see if they can mentally handle a meeting.

"And what is my job?" I asked him, although I was already sensing the answer.

"You know," he answered slowly. "Your job, from the beginning, has been to gather information, to organize it and to spread it. But the information itself is not important."

"Information is only knowledge," I said to him.

"That's right," Antarel answered. "The important thing is what you can do with knowledge by not keeping the accumulated information to yourself. The knowledge of the real history of the planet earth, the origin of man and the process that has allowed the continuation of his species, and a conscious continuation of the knowledge of the real time *of the universe is different than you have realized. A new reality awaits you where everything will be different. But you must understand it to be able to act in accordance with your forgotten role as engineers of creation. The expectation is that you will now wake up and build in this new time."*

"*I have some questions about this…*"

"*We know,*" Antarel answered, with a very human smile.

"*According to the messages we received from you, there is a gradual process of entry into that other reality. Is it exactly like that? Wouldn't it be a sudden change?*"

"*The real time of the Universe is transmitted to you as an idea so you can understand the multidimensionality in which we move,*" Antarel affirmed. "*There are different realities in space that would be impossible to explain to you. But the important thing to know is that you will be integrated into one of these states, which affects the fabric of the cosmos and which preceded the installation of an alternative timeline on Earth and the subsequent appearance of the human being. The timeline in which you have been moving, although true, is nonetheless artificial. It was established obeying other higher laws. Everything in the universe is order and symmetry. Nothing can be done that is not supported by the vast network.*

"*It has been a very long process, which we have monitored, that is involved with leaving artificial time in order to connect to universal real time, a path that will have its peak moment, according to your system of measurement, at the solstice on December 21 of this year 2012. The importance of that date is that it marks the point of no return, ensuring the transition towards what we have always been waiting for: the integration of the human race into the cosmic community. In other words, the date of December 21 signals a special moment, but it is not the definitive point of access to us. It is merely a coordinate from which you will begin to come to us. You will begin to merge into one and to truly understand the universe. Then, the scientists on Earth will see things they have never seen before. They will have to correct* their old theories about the cosmos. Over time, they will discover the true nature of space in which they live."

At that moment, I felt that Antarel was connecting his mind to mine, so that I could see how it was that they got to the region of Alpha Centauri. For a moment, I felt myself floating in the cosmos. In a second, I would understand, and I knew that there would be significant findings related to Antarel's world.

"I think that our scientists already perceive this," I said.

"But they have not said everything. Nor have they foreseen what comes next," assured the Apunian.

"What comes next?" I asked.

"The 're-dimensioning' of the connection. The scientists on the earth will detect unknown, interdimensional, and energetic phenomena, which will restate everything. The Earth will return to the 'mother of all things.' And, that gradual integration into the membrane of reality where we exist and flow will enable you to create new possibilities in our worlds of origin and even in us, as creatures. You will open a door. You will draw a path. Something that many of you still find impossible with all the injustices you see on Earth. But as we have told you previously, there is more light in you than what you imagine. You can do wonderful things. You are just asleep. That is why you must remember. The final moment of all will be to remember."

"Then, they will confirm that the transit of the Earth and the awakening of many people are on track?"

"Not only is it on the right track. It is already done," assured Antarel.

At that moment a figure came to my mind: 400 Years. It was as if the giant Apunian was trying to tell me something. He was projecting that figure to me, which I understood as the time humanity required to establish a new and luminous society of consciousness, and thus be integrated into a "cosmic community."

Then, all would be understood.

Ricardo González

The Solar Disks

In the middle of this valuable interview with Antarel, I decided to ask about the recent work we had carried out with the solar disks, a network of thirteen objects of power that are placed along energy spots on the planet, from Mount Shasta to Antarctica. One of the most celebrated disks is the one that the Incas were guarding at the Temple of the Sun or *Coricancha*, in Cusco. Legend claims that this golden disk remained there, until the Spanish conquest in the Sixteenth century. Then, it was taken by a group of initiated Incas and was carried into the jungle where the mythical Paititi or El Dorado dwells.[1] Behind this legend is the history of one of thirteen magnetic disks that function as windows into other realities.

Over the past ten years that I have been working with the solar disks, I have also continued with my questions to the extraterrestrial.

"You affirmed in your messages that the activation of the disks is complete. What comes after that?"

"It is important that you connect with the disks and centers of power where you are," Antarel spoke firmly. *"The disks are pulsating and their energy will accompany earth for a long time. The process of activation, in its preliminary stage, ended in August of this year."*

"But, Antarel," I interrupted the giant Apunian, *"why are there so many contradictions with the information of the disks? I do not doubt what you transmitted to us, but there are different visions circulating regarding what you revealed to me in Celea."*

And it was true. Since the extraterrestrials provided that information to me during the physical contact of 2001 in Perú, many spiritual groups around the world threw themselves into

---

[1] I tell this story and the legend of Paititi in my book, *Masters of Paititi*, reissued by Luciernaga Publishing of Grupo Planeta, Spain.

trying to locate the disks, seeking experiences in places where they might be hidden. The subject became so popular that alleged messages from extraterrestrials began to circulate, attributing certain qualities to the disks, changing their locations, and even changing the associated mantras that the extraterrestrials had originally given to us. And, as if that were not enough, travel agencies began to promote tours to places where these tools were located. I viewed this with much surprise because the revelation of the existence of these disks was not intended to turn the focus of our attention outward, but instead to help us understand that the focus of the work is inward.

"*Access to truthful, relevant information goes through different stages,*" Antarel said to me. "*Stages that involve questioning, confusion, verification, comprehension and, finally, its deep validation. The locations of the disks that we transmitted to you are correct, and you have done an outstanding job with the information. But, as we also have transmitted to you in messages, there are other mirrors that are in tune to the network we revealed to you.*"

At that time, another mental image came to me. It was the seminar group meditating in Shasta with the thirteen names of this network of power disks.

"*The most important thing that you have done with the disks,*" Antarel continued, "*has been to receive their tonal keys and transmit them to your brothers and sisters. Thousands of people are singing this vibration, which keeps the already active disks awake. But all this, also, will tune you into the sanctums of the White Brotherhood*[2]*. The sound of the disks opens doors of contact. Even for us.*"

According to Antarel and the extraterrestrial guides, the network of disks acts as a catalyst of our consciousness and intentions. Through the transmission of the tonal keys—the

---

[2]Beings of great power who spread spiritual teachings through selected humans. See page 116.

mantra of thirteen names—the network is connected and it maintains the pulse of the disks, which radiate outward and assist the Earth in its gradual process of transformation.

"*I understand,*" I said, thoughtfully. "*But, you have already seen many times where contradictions have overwhelmed me. If several people in the world are being connected, why is a different language perceived in everything you do?*"

"*Our message is consistent,*" Antarel answered firmly. "*The witnesses are the ones who interfere and pollute what we transmit. We are aware of it and it is a risk we take. Our hope is that over time, they can improve as channels and as vehicles for our communications. Therefore, in some messages, we are perceived as more mystical, in others more scientific. Sometimes, it happens because of the way the experience is interpreted. For us, in reality, what you call personality does not exist.*

"*It is true that each of us has a characteristic makeup of our unique subtle bodies and life experiences, and it is that we are learning from you. At times, we feel very human to you. But we are beyond the mirages of the mind.*"

"*Then, how do we avoid these interferences? What do you advise us to do?*"

"*Come to a greater understanding of how your mind functions,*" he asserted. "*You have already received sufficient information to train. It is also important to cultivate discernment and to be properly instructed.*"

"*The discernment to inquire? To investigate? I have always thought so, but, some might assume it would generate a subconscious 'contamination' of the messages.*"

"*If you start working with the mind, it will not,*" asserted Antarel. "*When you train the mind's ability it expand so that it can see a chain of information in perspective, this allows us to speak to you about other things.*"

"*And love? Where is it in all this?*"

"Remember what you have learned: The human being is pure by nature. And, his actions are what tune him in with love, the most powerful force of creation. Therefore, the test to overcome is not in the soul, which is a complete expression of love, but in the mind, which can be a major obstacle, or a great ally, depending on how it is educated."

"I have more questions Antarel!" I said standing up, facing the giant Apunian. I was trying to clear all possible doubt. *"The Chintamani Stone, will it soon return to the Universe? On the trip to Sajama, they also told us that the Thirty-Two would leave, what does this mean?"*

The extraterrestrial connection to the White Brotherhood

Throughout these years of contact, I can confirm that the extraterrestrials maintained a link with an advanced intraterrestrial society known in various mystical circles as the White Brotherhood. The existence of these enigmatic emissaries goes back to the legend of Shambhala in Central Asia, and to the survival of the knowledge of ancient priests, who fled with the records of their now extinct civilizations into underground shelters. The Hopi story we saw earlier, where beings from other worlds rescued people from a collapse into the ocean and then placed them in an underground base in Mount Shasta, is part of this story.

Moreover, in the experience of contact, we verified that many of the so-called "hot spots" of UFO sightings were next to enclaves associated with these elusive intra-terrestrial masters. They are the guardians of those thirteen disks of power and other objects that possess supernatural powers. The most important is the mythical Chintamani Stone, a crystal of extraterrestrial origin that was brought thousands of years ago to our world by The Thirty-Two Cosmic Masters. I imagine they are the same thirty-two Kings of Shambhala mentioned in the

Buddhist doctrine of *Kalachakra* (or Wheel of Time). The stone was the founding element of their legendary base on the Gobi Desert in Mongolia.

The existence of this crystal or something like it, has historically appeared in films around the world, yet it is well-kept knowledge in Buddhism and Hinduism. The famous painter, explorer and archeologist Nicholas Roerich, the Russian creator of the famous Banner of Peace, painted it in more than one picture at Chintamani and suggested, in his paintings, that it came from Orion.

Further, the design of the flag of Peace, recognized by the United Nations, was inspired by the cosmic stone.

"The main reason for this meeting, is to transmit the answers you need," Antarel said. *"But, it will not be by us. We have brought you here on behalf of someone else."*

Antarel stepped backwards a few steps and I saw that Anitac had closed her eyes while she was placing the black metal cube to her chest, holding it with her right hand and resting the palm of her left hand on it. The cube became transparent and, at that time, a distortion of the space in front of me began to happen, capturing my full attention. A bubble, as if made of water, was swelling up in the room, growing to a little over 1 meter in diameter.

I saw very clear images through that sort of plasma window that allowed me to perceive the faint silhouette of Antarel on the other side. Then, I recognized a mountain, which I had not yet visited, but knew through a "non-physical" experience I had had in the Gobi Desert. It was Mount Belukha, in Siberia.

The secret of Altai

I then noticed a large building of some sort, with a few crystal urns attached to its walls, and in the middle, at the end of this immense space, a huge chair of stone. It was the same room that I had seen in Gobi, after a projection into the ship of the Thirty-Two Cosmic Teachers hidden in Belukha.

An image of a face began to take shape. It was the face of an old imposing man with Nordic features and thin white hair, who I had seen before, during the same experience of Gobi. Only, this time, he had his eyes open, beautiful sky-blue eyes.

"Emuriel," I said, trembling with emotion.

"The announcement is very close." He spoke very slowly; I was listening to his powerful voice in my head. *"Our transformation is imminent and this will fulfill what we were waiting for."*

"Will you come back as the messages said?" I asked, still trembling at that moment, feeling overcome by the situation.

"We do not leave in the literal sense that you understand as in a departure. We have left the lead of the White Brotherhood on Earth to you. From other planes, we will continue to follow everything, but we will no longer be established in your world."

Emuriel is one of the thirty-two Cosmic Masters who came to Earth with the mission of bringing the crystal, which would generate a secure archive of all human history. Since the founding of Shambhala, thousands of years ago in Mongolia, they had remained physically alive thanks to a system of suspended animation, controlled by a program from their spaceship. They stood for thousands of years in that latent state within the Belukha massif, the highest mountain of the Altai Mountain range in Siberia. And–now, Emuriel was telling us that the time of his departure had come.

"And this will occur on September 21st?" I asked him.

"Yes, and it has been possible thanks to everything the humans have done. You have spread hope, demonstrating that we were not wrong in your potential. Our cycle is met, and yours begins."

I then saw another "holographic" image, one of the crystal, which had been located previously in the Gobi, and currently placed in Sajama mountain in the Bolivian Andes. This crystal is the Chintamani Stone, and sits surrounded by a blue, intense, beautiful light.

"The stone, the oracle will be read by humanity. It shows that the history of your future and ours, is written and evolves toward an understanding of its meaning and mission. Therefore, you see it changing from its original green color to blue: the color of the energy of the aura of your world. Your energy. This event joins our past with the future that you represent. It is also a portal. Understand this vision and share it with your brothers and sisters."

"When will the stone return to its place in the universe, where it originated?"

"It will take a while yet, but its return is guaranteed. It will carry the human experience, the energy of the Earth, to the Origin of the Universe, affecting the matrix, the source."

I asked, *"Is that crystal the one that will end up affecting creation?"*

"You, as living beings on this planet, with your feelings, your thoughts, and actions, are affecting the Universe. And, all that you do when connecting with this new reality will be even more influential for us, for everything. The crystal brings that information. It is a record. And it is part of what was programmed from the beginning.

"On September 21st," Emuriel continued, *"the beloved Master also taught us the way he will reveal himself, glorifying our bodies and the spaceship wherever we are. We will be transformed, when their presence is lit in the middle of us. Then, we will wake up, and will have fulfilled our task on the Earth."*

"You have spoken about Jesus. Are you saying Jesus will return?" I said suddenly, by impulse.

This is one of the most controversial issues that I have to confront with my contact experience: The mention of Jesus and other spiritual masters in human history. According to the extraterrestrials, they studied our civilization for a long time, and they say that they were amazed and moved by the lives of some characters, like Jesus. According to them, he was a real being, beyond the manipulated figure created by some religions, a human who lived in true love, and one whose steps opened a portal of understanding for the cosmic intelligences that were watching us. He would not have been a single revolutionary or zealot, as some texts attempted to minimize him. According to the beings of the cosmos, he was a different kind of human.

In addition, the extraterrestrials say that the birth and mission of Jesus was closely followed, as part of the program. Perhaps the descriptions of possible UFOs in the Bible such as the Star of Bethlehem, or the star over the cave where Jesus was born were reports of this program. A more complete story in the disputed apocryphal Gospels, leads us to consider a similar extraterrestrial presence at the time of Galileo.

Therefore, Jesus was not an ordinary human being. He had a connection with the universe or, if we put it another way, the *father* or *God*. He was linked to the source energy. According to the extraterrestrials, after his terrible death and subsequent resurrection, Jesus reached a level of glorification on Earth that ranks him as one of the most exemplary beings of the Universe.

It sounds incredible to hear it from them and it has been one of the most difficult issues for me to assimilate.

Yet, if all this was real, if Jesus and other great spiritual teachers from human history attracted the attention of the extraterrestrials to the point of becoming an example of evolution and consciousness for them, wouldn't this be the objective of the so called, Cosmic Plan? I must say that beyond my own doubts, and risking becoming a target in regard to this delicate topic in particular, thinking about him, in light of what I have learned from them, affects my faith very deeply. They, also, feel his power.

"*Jesus. I knew it!*" I said excited. "*But, how will it happen? How will this manifestation occur?*"

"*This is not the definitive return that he announced to you,*" Emuriel clarified. "*On the date that we have indicated to you, a fold will open, which will overlap two realities that will unite us to his presence, allowing his luminous visit in this place, where we rest. It is because He is the spiritual head of the White Brotherhood on Earth. The Lord of Love, Truth and Time.*"

Then, the cosmic being continued:

"*At that time, the first stars will light up the south half of the world, you will be able to feel his presence, if you open your heart. It does not matter where you are, but rather the harmony in which you are. 2,000 years ago, in your time, there were souls who saw him, and others that did not recognize him. The purity of heart, one of the most distinctive features of the human being, is the one characteristic that will allow humans to see him.*"

"*All of this is too much,*" I said, overwhelmed.

"*After this event,*" explained Emuriel, "*you must know that there will be another major fold that will close the process, a symbolic door which will open on December 21st. After you cross through, nothing will be the same. It is a door of consciousness, more than an inter-dimensional threshold. That day, you must be with the most important people to you. It will not take place where you are, but with who you are. It is an event that commemorates something ancient and that marks a new future, a different one that is built by your deepest feelings of Love and Brotherhood. In these words, you will find the key that day.*"

"*Will it no longer be necessary to go back to Gobi?*" I asked.

"The energies of the world find their focal point in the Andes. It is there where you should begin to meet for what is coming, but some of you will return to Gobi and other places in Asia, with other objectives."

"Emuriel, excuse my question, but what are the objectives? We need to know more to better understand."

"Remember, at some point, it was said to you that you had to know the truth to be part of it. Did you understand it? Do you want to see it? For this is also why you were brought here."

"I am ready," I said, having no idea what I would see. Antarel and Anitac remained silent, watching my interview with Emuriel.

The plasma bubble expanded, and I saw, as in a movie, many of the revelations to which we had had access in other experiences, such as ancient extraterrestrial visits to Earth, the story of the Chintamani stone and its origin in Orion, and the massive destruction of civilizations. This was followed by information about the White Brotherhood and I began to understand the process better. I began to understand how to explain those stories and the work that needed to be done. Everything that was coming was different.

I spent several minutes watching and absorbing the images, until a scene shocked me. I saw Mount Belukha, and an underground place, that was not the spaceship of the Thirty-Two. I saw another site that seemed to have been built in a huge cave inside the large mountain of Altai. There, I saw other glass cases and, within them, humanoid, extraterrestrial bodies in perfect condition. They were not cryopreserved as was the case of the Thirty-Two. Why did they preserve these bodies?

"They are the martyrs," I heard Emuriel's voice. I had been hearing the voice of Emuriel, while I was immersed in these images.

"They came from the stars long ago, and now are on Earth, living the human experience and helping in the transition."

"Why do we preserve the bodies?" I asked with some anxiety.

"For this reason you will go to Altai. You will complete another episode of information. And there you will know it."

This statement was ringing in my mind, while I was contemplating the face of one of those extraterrestrial beings; a face that looked familiar. And, then I received the date of the trip: August, 2014.

Suddenly, I was no longer looking through the plasma bubble. It was as if it had grown and I was inside of it. I was there! I was no longer on the spaceship with the guides.

What is happening? I asked myself, my heart pounding.

"I am here," I heard Emuriel's voice say.

Then, I understood. I was in the building I had initially seen in the bubble. Inside the spaceship of the Thirty-Two. It was no longer a vision. I was there!

There was a strange silence, even sharper than that of Antarel's ship. I could breathe perfectly and I could see everything with clarity, since the place was illuminated. I walked towards the crystal urn that I had already seen, and inside it I found, in suspended animation, Emuriel!

"Tell everyone that they must be united, that they must trust in everything that they can do. You are here on behalf of your brothers, and as on other occasions, the message will come to whom it is destined. Do not worry about anything. You are not alone. Now, go, return."

And, in an instant, I was again standing in the center of Antarel's ship

Antarel was looking at me with an expression of a completely human joy. Anitac was holding the black cube that had become solid again in her right hand. As we will see later on, this mysterious artifact would have an important role during the experience of April 12, 2015 in the Peruvian Andes.

I couldn't believe it! How did they do that? Did they open a portal inside the ship itself?

"You never moved from here," Antarel said, smiling. "You were there, but you did not move from here."

"Wasn't it real?" I asked, confused.

"It was real, but you did not move from the spaceship, you were always with us. That is what we explained to you earlier about the dimensional gates."

"It seemed like the Xendra," I said.

"Yes, but this was another type of experience," Antarel hurried to explain. "And, you will understand later on. Do not forget that you are multidimensional beings. We have only precipitated something artificially that you can achieve without technology, once you have awakened."

"It is time that you return," Antarel continued. "Your brothers of the group wait for you. We have been with them."

Somehow, I knew that this experience was proceeding with the presence and involvement of three spaceships. I was in one of them and the other two were over Sand Flat, on Shasta.

"You know, we also have a base here," Antarel said, as he slowly approached me. "Starting next year, there will be another period of silence, so there won't be any physical interviews," he said. "You must already know that to arrange a direct meeting with you, there are a number of mechanisms that are beyond our control."

"I am going to miss you," I said, a little sad.

"Only for a while, you will not see us, but we will continue to follow you. We will maintain communication and you will have evidence of our presence. But, now you must focus on what is coming. You hold enough information to know what to do."

Then, the giant Apunian put his huge right hand on my left shoulder, and said, "We are going to leave you on the ground. Close your eyes, so that the glow will not harm your sight. Inside here, it is *stronger. When you no longer feel my hand on your shoulder, it will be time. Ready?"*

I didn't want to tell him I was ready. I wanted to feel a little more. Meanwhile, Anitac, who had been silent throughout the experience, smiled, as if she was saying goodbye.

"We are always with you," Antarel told me again. *"The energy of this experience will be with you to remind you of all that which has been shown to you, our conversations, and what you have felt. Rest, because you have to assimilate what you have experienced in this encounter, but then write it down and share it. Those who read of your experience with us will feel as if they had been here. They will vicariously experience this contact, because, through you, we have spoken to everyone. See you soon, beloved brother."*

I closed my eyes and told him in a loud voice, "Ready!"

Back at Sand Flat

As soon as Antarel removed his hand from my shoulder, a powerful glow penetrated me and I felt a sharp downward movement. In an instant, they had placed me back at Sand Flat.

I appeared on the ground, unbalanced, dizzy, and felt a sense of impressive bewilderment. I hardly recognized the place. My experience in the spaceship had been so real that the Shasta forest now felt like a dream.

I didn't know where to go and I could hardly walk. My body shook with a very weird feeling of nausea and my head ached. The discomfort was only physical; I was emotionally happy. I was filled with light. I was happy and grateful for everything—the group, my life, for everything. A positive energy of brotherhood stayed with me after my visit with my guides.

The sound of the group chanting guided me back to my companions. When I arrived, they saw me in a different way. Many did not recognize me.

Some even thought that I was one of the guides. They recognized me only when I was closer to them. Raul Dominguez hugged me and helped me, because he saw my difficulty walking. Everyone in the group excitedly hugged me, too. Moved, I thanked them for continuing to meditate and chant during my contact experience. I thought I had been gone for around an hour and a half. But, they told me said I had been absent for about 15 to 20 minutes. I told them that was impossible, but Raul checked his watch, and it was only 9:25 pm. Then, everyone checked their watches and cell phones and confirmed that, in fact, less than an hour had passed.

I was exhausted and sat while they told me that the first spaceship they saw at 9:00 pm spent several minutes with them and then, a second spaceship arrived, which stopped above the group and accompanied them during a part of the work. They also saw another object moving in the sky above me, when I came walking towards them.

I shared with them what had happened, as best I could, relaying to them some of the things that the extraterrestrials had transmitted to me, including the "interdimensional interview" with Emuriel within the spaceship itself. When I told them about Antarel touching my chest, a new spaceship appeared behind me and everyone saw it. When Luis Ochoa, heard my story about the children I found in the forest, the "hologram" that the extraterrestrials created to help calm me, he told me that earlier in the afternoon, in Shasta, he had fallen asleep in his truck and had a dream in which saw a similar group of children. As he watched them, a being said to him, *"Take care of the children."*

After a short while, I told the group that our work was done and that we could go. At that moment, one last spaceship appeared, very bright and large It's light spread above the pine forest.

It was amazing.

There was another very special moment during our closing gratitude meditation to the *guides* for their support. Another very strong wind struck the group as if it was sweeping us clean. It felt as if it was generated by something from above, for just an instant, and then all went still.

Before we got into the truck, Lorena Dominguez hugged me and said, "I want to feel the energy of the guides, now that you have been with them." Minutes later, Lorena was experiencing a subtle dizziness and a headache, which kept her from work on Monday. Some group members that night felt very thirsty and dehydrated. We all were in a kind of shock. In my case, it took me a significant time to assimilate this experience.

Inside the ship, Antarel had touched upon many topics during our conversation. He had discussed key points that allowed us to understand our work in the future. All of the things Antarel announced in the contact would, in time, come to pass.

Contact From Planet Apu

Chapter 8

EXOPOLITICS: THE INVITATION TO MICHAEL SALLA

On September 21, 2012, following the recommendation of the extraterrestrials, an international group went to Talampaya, in Argentina, to connect remotely to Mount Belukha in the Altai. It was the location where the thirty-two Cosmic Teachers physically abandoned Earth, after they had remained in material bodies for a long time with humanity. After this transformation, they continued assisting men from other planes of consciousness.

In Talampaya, we had beautiful experiences as soon as the extraterrestrials presented themselves through various sightings, at the exact time they had indicated. It was a true "communion" with them on that trip.[1]

On October 16th, a scientific news report reminded me of the experience with Antarel on Shasta: A team of European astronomers had discovered a planet with a mass somewhat larger than Earth, orbiting a star in the Alpha Centauri system.

It also the lightest exoplanet found so far orbiting around a sun-like star about six million kilometers away. According to the Reuters wire agency's own website and NASA[2], that world was discovered by the HARPS instrument, which is installed

---

[1] In my book Talampaya, the Other Story of Erks (Ecis Publications, Buenes Aires, 2013) I detail the different experiences we have had in that Argentinian area.
[2] http://www.nasa.gov/home/hqnews/2012/oct/HQ_12-366_NASA_Statement_Alpha_Centauri.html

in the telescope of the La Silla (La Silla meaning the chair) Observatory in the Atacama region in Chile.

"Four years of observations have yielded little more than a tiny signal, but a real one, of a planet orbiting Alpha Centauri B every 3.2 days," said Xavier Dumusques[3], of the Geneva Observatory (Switzerland) and the Center for Astrophysics at the University Porto (Portugal) and lead author of the study.

"This result represents a major step towards the detection of a twin planet to Earth in the immediate vicinity of the Sun. We live in exciting times," said the scientist, adding, "It is an extraordinary discovery and has led our technology to its limits!"

While it is true that scientists estimate that the surface temperatures near Alpha Centauri would be too high to support life, as we know it, they also think that this planet must be part of a solar system that itself would hold some promise. Are our scientists searching for the world the Apunians colonized near Alpha Centauri? Was this finding made at the Atacama observatory part of a program or at least related to the already mentioned Longshot Project? We were later to understand.

I was in Peru on December 21, 2012. While some fanatics took refuge in their bunkers awaiting a planetary catastrophe, such as the messianic ascension of the planet into a fourth or fifth dimension, Sol and I and a group of old friends were gathered in the Chilca desert. We had decided to go to the desert to meditate for world peace and reflect on the message of this new historical stage that mankind began after the end of the Mayan Long Count—a sacred cycle of 5,125 years. According to Mayan knowledge, the *big wheel* is composed of thirteen Baktuns. The elders of that culture, a culture that is still alive in Mexico

---

[3]In an article published by the newspaper, *La Vanguardia*, October 17, 2012.

and Central America, argue that the solstice of December 21st ended Baktun 13, starting Baktun 14 or Gate 14. A Baktun is a cycle of 144,000 days, or approximately 400 solar years, which fits perfectly with the future time frame Antarel helped me understand, when I was taken onboard the spaceship.

On this trip to Peru, I met by chance, though I do not believe in coincidences, Michael E. Salla, who as I mentioned, is a senior UFO researcher and founder of the Exopolitics movement. Dr. Salla, through Giorgio Piacenza, the Italian-Peruvian scholar, published a report about my Shasta contact experiences in the *Exopolitics Journal*. My testimony had caused great interest among English readers, but, as expected, I was viewed with suspicion by some UFO researchers. I do not blame them; what happened to me in Shasta, the interview with Antarel and everything I was told seemed crazy. But it was real.

It might be helpful, here, to explain some of my history with Michael Salla.

In 2008, through our friend Monica Robles, I received an invitation to attend a UFO conference in Hawaii, organized by Dr. Salla. It was Salla himself who organized it. However, I could not attend due to previous commitments.

I must also say that I was not interested in Exopolitics. I had already participated in several meetings and conferences with researchers of that movement who did not quite convince me. Among the people with whom I participated was Alfred Lambremont Webre (former adviser to US President Jimmy Carter); but, as I say, I did not quite understand some theories and assertions of that initiative that looked for ways to address contact with advanced societies of other worlds.

But, circumstances conspired and I finally met with Dr. Salla in 2012 in my own country.

We met in a hotel in Miraflores, where Dr. Salla asked me to invite him to a scheduled sighting in Shasta. Dr. Salla wanted to be an objective witness to any physical action, such as a scheduled sighting. My initial reaction was that I did not want to do it, but a brief statement from Antarel was going to make me change my mind.

Shortly thereafter, during a workshop taught in Asuncion, Paraguay, the Apunian guide told me in a telepathic message, *"Do not doubt. Invite Salla to Mount Shasta, we will be there. It is important. The contact will be on Saturday August 3, between 9 and 10 pm."*

It was after hearing this message that I became determined to do it and I had many confirmations and encouragement to speak to Piacenza and Dr. Salla about the scheduled sighting at Mount Shasta.

To add validity to the invitation from Antarel to Dr. Salla, I publicly announced the scheduled contact on Chilean television on a program called, True Lies. This public statement was made more than a month in advance of the event in Shasta, specifying that Salla was invited.

That scheduled sighting would be very important. As I said, Dr. Michael Salla is a pioneer in the development of Exopolitics, which he defines as "the study of the key actors, institutions and processes associated with extraterrestrial life." His interest in Exopolitics evolved from the research of international conflicts, and its relationship with an extraterrestrial presence that has been kept from the public, elected officials and even high-ranking military officers.

Although I have always kept aloof of this movement, I must say that Dr. Salla is an internationally recognized scholar in international politics. He is the author of several books on the subject and he has authored more than seventy articles, chapters and book reviews on peace, ethnic clashes and conflict resolution. He was an adviser to President Ronald Reagan. He has a Doctorate from the University of Queensland in Australia, and a Master of Philosophy from the University of Melbourne and has many more experiences that testify to his credibility. He has conducted research and fieldwork on ethnic conflicts in East Timor, Kosovo, Macedonia and Sri Lanka; he has also organized peace initiatives involving middle to high-level participants from those conflicts. Recently, he has become a full-time UFO researcher and to be numbered as a contact witness with Dr. Salla is a unique fact.

I knew Antarel and our star brothers would not fail us. The spaceships appeared at the scheduled time. In fact, there were four UFOs and a message to Dr. Salla. We had four very clear sightings of objects that moved at low altitude, and interacted with more than 50 witnesses, including Dr. Salla and Piacenza.

The aliens were prompt and forceful. The ships quickly crossed the group vertically, in sinuous lines while accelerating and decelerating at will. One of these objects even interrupted its trajectory and remained fixed in the sky for a few moments. It was impossible to capture it with our cameras due to its position and to the darkness of the night.

Another object appeared, flying much lower than a commercial airliner, and as the entire group watched, the UFO lit up with intensity, in a beautiful bright, white light.

At that moment, I felt Antarel nearby, and the need arose to receive a telepathic, automatic-writing communication. I asked the group for their support. Dr. Salla, perplexed, observed everything. No sooner had I asked for support from the group to receive the message then there appeared behind my location (northeast) a very bright object. It seemed to be parked at very low altitude, almost on the horizon. It was close. It was a manned spacecraft. We all saw it. I relaxed and began to receive the following message:

> Mount Shasta, August 3, 2013
> 9:55 pm.
>
> Yes, we are the ones.
>
> You have been able to confirm our presence with this scheduled sighting.
>
> We have presented ourselves to provide our support, so as not to lose the strength to move forward.
>
> Contact with us is real. But more important is what lies below the surface: our relationship with you.
>
> We have a message for Michael Salla: we want you to know our true intentions of the light. He must understand our positive stance and our interest in contact and sharing the experience with humans.
>
> We will support you in this effort.
>
> Contact has been established. You will see changes, and there will be major events.
>
> Pay attention.
> —Antarel

After this extraordinary contact at Mount Shasta, Dr. Salla shared his testimony with different news media.

In addition, we were interviewed by different TV channels and radio programs. Among them was the renowned NBC-Telemundo, a US chain that allowed us to talk via satellite nationwide in the United States and 27 other countries.

On August 23rd, in Napa Valley, California, Antarel communicated once again and among other things he said:

"We have been very close since the scheduled meeting in Mount Shasta. We presented ourselves at the agreed meeting time in order to strengthen the message you are spreading, and to persuade Michael Salla. In the future, they will have a better picture, and they will see what comes next. We are sowing change in the paradigms that some still have about us and our intentions.

"We reiterate our friendship guidance and counseling to help them remember who they are and where they are going." –Antarel

From this experience, I began to see Exopolitics in a new light. I realized that the idea of studying all significant variables of contact with an advanced extraterrestrial society was a positive thing, very different from the outrageous conspiracy theories that gave a distorted view in the UFO world.

The contact experience with Dr. Michael Salla was an attempt to change the basic idea regarding the phenomenon of UFOs and extraterrestrial life abductions, cattle mutilations, military conspiracies, and so on. Antarel wanted the true facts to be known about them and that there are beings in the universe that are ethical and respectful of us. They desire contact with us and, in the future, we will be members of this cosmic family.

Contact From Planet Apu

Chapter 9

PAOLA HARRIS AND A GROUP CONTACT WITH ANTAREL

Saturday, August 2, 2014 Siberia, Russia. Our expedition group left behind the captivating figure of Mount Belukha, a magical and memorable stay after several days camping in its vicinity. We fulfilled the extraterrestrials invitation that was given to us in the contact of 2012 on Mount Shasta.

Our walk back was very arduous. We were descending towards the main base camp, located in Vysotnik. We were about 30 miles from the point that would allow us to take a vehicle to Barnaul, the city and administrative center of Altai Krai, located in the south of Western Siberia. We had at least two days to hike up to Vysotnik.

During the intense day, with heavy backpacks in tow, I reflected about everything that we had experienced in Yarlu and Akkem. My mind, at the time, traveled to Shasta. The pine forests in the Altai were very similar to the landscape that one can see at the foot of the magic Mount Shasta, in California. The same supernatural presence was felt. Perhaps this connection was what hooked me up with a message that burst suddenly into my mind: *"We will be at Mount Shasta. Invite Paola Harris. It is important."*

Without difficulty, I could identify this message from Antarel. But, despite the clarity of it, and the very manifestation of extraterrestrial guides over our camp during one of the breaks on the way back, I was reluctant to take the suggestion of the extraterrestrials. Do I again invite a journalist, to take part in our contact experiences? It had been hardly a year since the successful scheduled sighting with Dr. Michael Salla. What drove the extraterrestrials to arrange a new meeting at the foot of the mountain in the United States?

I left Russia with these questions. And a few days later, in Spain, Antarel restated the invitation to Harris in a message I received in Malaga, on August 10, 2014:

Prepare yourself for Shasta where we will show ourselves. And you may invite Paola Harris. We do so to continue supporting your sustained efforts to disseminate the message and to promote a more realistic view of our intentions to help humans. We are one.

Love,
Antarel

As had happened before with Dr. Salla, this message from Antarel gave me the reassurance to invite Paola Harris. It would be the fifth time that a journalist or researcher would participate in contact experiences.

And, Harris is a special case. She is a field journalist and researcher specializing in Ufology. She has followed the UFO subject, since 1979. She worked for several years with Dr. Joseph Allen Hynek the father of ufology, astronomer and scientific advisor to Project Blue Book, who was also a consultant for the screenplay and film, Close Encounters of the Third Kind. He was someone who had interviewed the most illustrious UFO witnesses from military, Vatican prelates, and defense ministers. Harris is the author of several books, a speaker at numerous conferences on this subject, and is considered one of the most important UFO researchers worldwide. To have her at Shasta would be a real honor, as well as a tremendous responsibility.

After the message from Antarel, I contacted the group from Altai to notify them that the guides would be in Shasta, with Paola Harris as a witness. Uncertain of what might happen, we decided to be cautious with the message and not generate an overflow of people on the mountain.

So, On September 16, just four days before the meeting in Shasta, we closed up the camp and communicated all this information.

Originally, we chose September 20 and 21 for the International Day of Peace. We would not have imagined that Antarel would signal this meeting for a new contact.

"Ricardo, I feel that a *Xendra* will open in Shasta," Raymundo Collazo of the United States said, as we talked by video conference about the invitation of the Apunians to Paola Harris. He added, "And I feel like Paola will enter that *Xendra*."

I confess that the perception of Raymundo struck me. Raymundo, a fellow expeditioner, had always been perceptive and practical. I thought about his words and began to sense that Harris might, in addition to a researcher and reporter, become a contactee.

After our conversation, I had several dreams influenced by our discussion. I saw a small group entering the Xendra, and I went to find Paola Harris to take her to the door.

In the dreams, Paola seemed nervous, but brave, as she went with the group toward the concentration of energy. When I woke up, I shared my impressions with my partner Sol. I said that I had seen her within the Xendra, but that I was staying out of that energy, supporting her. Sol was confident that she would participate in such a contact. Soon, confirmations came. Alejandro Szabo, a cardiologist in Chile, and companion on the trip to Altai, sent me a message on August 14th. The message confirmed the intuition of Raymundo about the Xendra on Mount Shasta:

"On Shasta, in September, there will be a connection to the memory of those who attend. It has to do with what you experienced in

the Altai. The cosmos siblings will assist not only physically, but also in personal and group experiences. You will be surprised. There will be Xendra experiences at night. Ricardo must be careful. Everything will be coordinated." –Emuriel

Then Corinna Muzi, a young Italian anthropologist who also participated in the trip to Altai, wrote me and told me that the *guides* had also spoken of a *Xendra* at Shasta. Additionally, Fernando Lopez, a young entrepreneur from Mexico and another expeditioner in Siberia, informed us that he had a sighting over his home in Guadalajara, next to his parents' home on Thursday September 11th. Following that sighting, he received a message in which the extraterrestrials confirmed a Xendra would appear at Shasta. Six days later, Alexander, during his flight to the United States, made a drawing of the seven people who entered the *Xendra*, coinciding perfectly with dreams and previous perceptions that we already had.

Carlos Quintanilla, from one of the contact groups in Los Angeles, oblivious to all of this, contacted me and told me that during a camp held in Shasta with a small group, he had received a telepathic message that in our encounter a dimensional door would open. Confirmations began to arrive from everywhere!

As I said, before this scenario, we decided to be careful not to raise expectations. At the meeting, we would focus on peace meditations. I thought that if that door of light did open, we would proceed naturally and harmoniously in that moment. And so it was.

Antarel and the threshold of light

We camped at Shasta beginning the afternoon of September 19. Paola Harris arrived that day, accompanied by Raymundo and a beautiful group of people from Las Vegas (Nevada), who met her at the Sacramento airport. Our base was once again in the Sand Flat, the 1.2 mile high esplanade, with its view of the mountains. More than 160 people from different countries had gathered there.

It was a pleasure to meet Paola in person. Despite her busy schedule as a researcher of the UFO phenomenon, she attended the meeting as part of the group. She was very nice to everyone, simple, nice and humble. She has great charisma, intensity and passion for what she does. I have no hesitation in saying: when I hugged her, I felt I had known her forever.

That night, the group that came to Shasta witnessed two sightings. The guides of the cosmos were beginning to show themselves. Then, I received a telepathic message from Antarel, which I shared with the group that was present and then I repeated the same message to the whole camp on the morning of the 20th:

"Antarel tells me the night of the 20th, at 8:30 pm, there will be a closer visit by them that all will be able to verify. At that time, our specific work will start at midnight of the 21st, resulting in a chain of radiation for peace."

My intention was not to create expectations, but to simply explain what would happen. Paola followed everything that was happening closely.

Thus, between lectures, meditations and all kinds of energy work, we were constantly busy all the time until the appointed time: 8:30 pm.

I talked to all participants of the meeting asking them to remain calm before the sightings, and to learn to distinguish between things such as satellites, Iridiums, and typical flares, or the passage of the ISS (International Space Station), which was not visible that night on Shasta according to NASA. The night was crisp, with a beautiful blanket of stars, and a waning moon at just 9% of its luminosity.-

It all began at 8:30, as announced. The extraterrestrial sightings were impressively accurate and specific. First, it was a luminous object that drew a circuitous path in the sky, accompanied by another spaceship, flying in parallel. The first object then accelerated, while breaking formation, which drew applause from the crowd. Harris, watched attentively.

Fernando López soon became the chronicler of these spacecraft appearances. He could capture the sightings at least three times better with night vision equipment (Yukon Ranger Pro). I must say that Fernando was very clever, because the system LCD, which is added to the binoculars infrared, had just been ruined and therefore he could not record what the camera captured; however, Fernando solved the problem by adapting his cell phone to the equipment. He was able to film everything the night vision gear focused on. It reproduced faithfully what everyone saw—the ships, surrounded by bright lights, crossing the starry sky. It was important to have this device, to obtain better reference of the brightness and position of objects in the sky, something that is very difficult to capture with because it wasn't possible to get a faithful record with conventional cameras (because of its low sensitivity to light, which ends up reducing the object on a white point and off the stars, or reference element, on a black background).

After these sightings, we all gathered in the center of the Sand Flat for further meditation practices, mostly walking in silence, alone, for the vast expanse of the flat. It is a way to connect with yourself and be inspired by the bewitching forest of Shasta. We began a new practice to radiate peace to the planet. Aloud, I asked the extraterrestrials for another manifestation of their spaceships to confirm that we still remained on for the *Xendra* that they promised. We chanted the mantra, ZinUru, a word contained in the esoteric text The Emerald Tablets, attributed to Thoth or Hermes Trismegistus. That mantra means "key" and makes possible a connection between yourself and other realities. We didn't have to wait long. As soon as we started to repeat the mantra, a ship lit up in the night sky, just above us, and began to move toward a particular area of Shasta.

We didn't manifest the spaceship by our chanting, it had simply emerged as a response to our request. The mantras and meditations, as I said, are just techniques to bring a group of witnesses together.

The light was very strong, and Fernando recorded its appearance. Part of the appearance of this object he pointed out with a laser beam. It was awesome. In the video, all of this can be seen and the group can be heard in the background, vocalizing.

Seeking confirmation of what I had asked the *guides*, I suggested that all participants of the meeting wait in the base camp. Then, I talked to Raymundo and people from the group who were aware that I wanted to confirm the message about the *Xendra*. Wasting no time, the group of us, who were involved in this part of the sighting, went looking for the door of light. We went in the direction the trajectory of the spaceships had indicated. Interestingly, it was the same place where I was taken inside the spaceship during the experience of August 26, 2012.

We came to a clearing in the forest, where you could perfectly see an illuminated area. We turned off all the electronic equipment we had brought with us, including flashlights. The extraterrestrials themselves have recommended this, when one is next to a dimensional portal.

Although there was next to no moon that night, it was amazing how the area was lit. It was like a bright carpet that seemed to rise a few inches from the ground. Raymundo and I went on ahead, where we found the *Xendra*. Fernando, Sol, Corinna and Alexander were behind us. Suddenly, from the middle of that concentrated energy, we were hit with a feeling.

A presence. We stopped, but Fernando and Sol continued walking toward a person standing in the forest.

Excited, they saw a huge figure, ahead of them and to their right. This figure was not translucent or brilliant. It was solid and real and standing right in front of us. We all saw him.

At that moment, I clearly heard a voice in my head that said, *"Yes, brother, I am Antarel. Stop here."* Immediately, I warned Fernando and Sol to stop. They were about 20 feet from the giant Apunian.

Amid the energy and the unforgettable starry night, you could perfectly see the silhouette of this giant of nearly ten-feet tall. He was dressed in a close fitting suit of a very dark blue-gray. His hair was long and white, perfectly visible. He stood up straight, arms resting on either side, his face straight toward us. At that time, no one thought to take pictures. We were overcome by the moment and filled with joy. The group, with Fernando and Sol in front, stood before Antarel, who was physically located within the Xendra.

A moment later, Antarel stepped back and appeared to vanish into the woods. According to Fernando and Sol, who were closer, the extraterrestrial of Alpha Centauri didn't step back, but instead rose slightly, levitating. (This situation reminded me of a similar physical contact that I experienced in 2003 at the foot of another volcano like Shasta: Licancabur Atacama in Chile/Bolivia.) I went back to the camp to look for Paola, Suyapa, and Mercedes. This was just like the dream I had before this meeting in Shasta, and, as in the dream, I was following the instructions received from the *guides*.

I asked everyone from the camp for their support. Although we were a very large and heterogeneous group, there was no disorder from rushing to find Antarel. Everyone understood the situation perfectly and fulfilled their part. They supported our group of seven people while we went into that energy to meet Antarel on behalf of everyone.

Harris was thrilled. She was sensible, as in my dream, but also firm and attentive at all times. When we arrived at the scene, Harris was able to verify the potent energy that was there, and confirm how it was perfectly visible.

"Wow!" she exclaimed, when she saw the bright white light that illuminated the clearing.

Carlos Quintanilla, from Los Angeles, came with us as well. In this manner, the team that entered the Xendra consisted of Paola Harris, Suyapa Reyes (Honduran, from Napa Valley); Mercedes Gonzáles (Peruvian, from Las Vegas); Raymundo Collazo (Uruguayan, from Atlanta); Fernando López (México), Sol Sanfelice (Argentina) and Corinna Muzi (Italy). Alejandro stayed outside the energy to provide support.

As I mentioned, a *Xendra* is basically an artificial concentration of energy that allows dimensional experiences at different levels. These portals, according to what the extraterrestrials have told me, are not entirely physical. They function more as holographic environments where a person can be projected to another place, or receive information packets complete with guidelines and instructions for the short time they are within that energy.

And that is what happened on Shasta. The extraterrestrials opened a *Xendra* for us and our group went through this threshold. All of the ones who entered experienced something different or received significant personal revelations. For example, they showed Fernando the bond we have with old extraterrestrial civilizations. Suyapa experienced a great sense of confidence. She said she sensed someone who was very caring. She saw herself suspended in a place without space or time. She said she felt a strong pressure to the forehead, as if someone had put something in her head. Raymundo had someone place a foreign matter in his hands, a blue energy. For Corinna, they caused her to reflect on all that she had lived in the Altai, and the importance of continuing to work for peace. She also told the rest of us that the next step would be the world meeting in January 2015, on the outskirts of Capilla del Monte, Argentina.

For Harris, her main objective was to feel and she said that she thought someone was watching her from the woods. She knew that it was Antarel. Harris saw him. At first, I was afraid the impact of the experience was too big for her. While watching the giant Apunian, standing in the woods, Harris heard strange sounds, like an echo or radio communication, comparable to an unintelligible language that came from nowhere.

Sol also reported the same phenomenon. And, Mercedes experienced the same kind of communication with Antarel, feeling that the extraterrestrial watched everything from the forest. According to Harris, the sounds she heard were transformed finally into a phrase, in perfect English that she did not hear in her head, but with her ears as it came from the woods. A phrase came from where Antarel was. Simple and powerful, the phrase was, Thank you.

Paola sent an email to me, reviewing her report of the contact she wrote:

"...Antarel spoke constantly in a strange language, perhaps the mysterious Irdin. I could not understand. He had a voice with an echo, as if it were a radio transmission. I made a very big effort to listen and understand his words, coming from the top of the trees, to the right of my location. After a few minutes, two words were very, very clear. Thank you. He spoke in perfect English. They were perfect and clear words, they came accompanied by the echo...

"This was real contact. I felt that the 'Thank you' was for all of us. It meant that there is no separation."

After that, Harris received another message that she prefers to keep private.

She told me later, "This experience changed my life." She added, "Richard, do not worry so much about inviting journalists and researchers to corroborate the contacts. This is real. Concentrate on moving forward because there is no time to lose."

Paola's recommendation brought to my mind a message that Antarel had sent me in Santiago de Chile, exactly on February 23, 2014. The message I received in Chile said:

"...You will share these experiences of interaction with an audience that will open their hearts to our friendship. You must understand that the corroboration of contact, having as witnesses researchers and journalists will soon be anecdote. The message, as you know, is another. We are interested in having a closer relationship with prepared groups who are sensitive to our presence. When you summon us, we will be there brother." –Antarel

Harris' presence at this contact was a watershed moment, after which everything changed.

There is more that I remember about our time that night. When the group of seven left the *Xendra*, sparks formed around our heads and Alejandro, Carlos and I could see Antarel again, in another part of the forest. The Apunian guide was watching us from a distance. I sensed he was pleased with the outcome of this group contact.

"Do not stop trusting us, we are always with you," my older brother from the stars told me.

"This is just the beginning," Alexander heard in his mind.

Carlos Quintanilla, observing Antarel, heard, *"Michael (Salla), in addition to his own work, and Paola should join hands to work together. "*

When the group of seven left the *Xendra*, a bright flash appeared, as if the door was closing. It was so strong that some people from base camp, despite the distance, saw the strange glow.

Upon returning to the camp, there was something else. Antarel started talking to me, telepathically. As it was happening, I forwarded the message to the group. It was as if the Apunian was in our midst. It was very special.

Below is a transcription of the audio captured by Carlos Gomez at that moment.

> *I'm feeling the presence of Antarel again. And he tells me to convey this message to all of you.*
>
> *They are very happy with our presence here in the mountains and they appreciate how we have been able to accomplish this in the midst of our personal lives and find a point of equilibrium and balance. He says that they have been watching closely. Many of you have felt this, beyond the presence of the spaceships in the sky. But Antarel clarifies that they care more than what we may feel. They yearn for peace for planet Earth. And he says that we ought to see them as friends, and that we should understand that they cannot always show themselves openly to everyone, as they have a strict program that limits their contact. However, where possible, they try to approach us.*
>
> *Antarel says that they like our human energy, our emotions; to some extent they identify with the humans, as we have seen when we cry, laugh, worry about all sorts of things. He says that the way we live and feel are emotions that their civilization has lost. For that reason, they see us as their past and, at the same time, their future. They want you to know (Antarel is not alone, there is a group with him) that you are not abandoned,*

that they are not alien to us: we are part of one family, and they are currently here with us.

Antarel says, "Feel our presence, because we also accompany you in your work for world peace. Right now, we are stationed vertically above your group. We can see you in the circle you have formed. We can feel your thoughts, personal fears, doubts, but we also feel your joy. You are so diverse and wonderful. And, special. Sensing your thoughts does not mean that we are spying. We are simply connected to each creature and we see that you are looking for something important, something that we, in our home worlds, have always sought.

"We seek peace and fraternal coexistence, but our pride became more important than our knowledge of the Universe and made us lose an important contact with the spirit, with the essence of things. We had psyched everything. And today, seeing how diverse your thoughts are, how different you are, and especially how wonderful you are, we understand that there is hope.

"We say thanks to everyone and even though you see us as extraterrestrial teachers, we are not so different from you. You help us to believe in something immense. Something that will affect you and our civilizations.

"As you know, many of us have left or lost our home worlds, traveling far to Earth. We live from base to base, whether in orbit or installed in secret places in your world. We lost the consciousness of Home. But, today we feel that the Earth is our home, and we say this with much respect. We also feel part of the global peace, because everything that happens in your world affects us. We say goodbye. Do not forget that we will always be brothers.

"Love,
"Antarel"

Contact From Planet Apu

Chapter 10

Huascarán: Apunian Base

In November of 2014, I participated, by invitation from Paola Harris, in an important UFO conference in Laughlin, Nevada. There, Harris shared her Mt Shasta experience. In my opinion, she did the right thing, making public and describing our contact with the Apunians. I was the only Latin American contactee in that conference, which was held at the Aquarius Casino Resort. My talk was well-received and ended with a large public standing ovation, which was quite emotional, due to the message I delivered from the Apunians.

In December, already in Buenos Aires, I met with the contact group that seeks out direct communication, with the extraterrestrials. By suggestion of the brothers of the cosmos, we were organizing a meditation on behalf of world peace in the outskirts of Capilla del Monte. This is a picturesque Argentinean town, located at the edge of the mythic Urritorco hill, famous worldwide for its UFO sightings. Our intention was to ask some details, guidelines and recommendations for such a meeting.

The message I received in our meeting according to my notebook, at 8:00 pm on December 29, 2014, began intriguingly as follows:

"Yes," he wrote, *"I am Antarel."*

"We are sending this message from our underground base located in the heart of Huascarán. That mountain hides one of our oldest facilities on Earth. As you know, the location of that base was connected with our first contact in Peru. You will come back to that region of the Andes that you visited in your youth."

Huascarán? I hadn't visited there for nearly 20 years, but the extraterrestrials never leave anything to chance."

What was I to make of this invitation? I knew there was an intent to mention this base situated in the great Andean snow.

Huascarán (to the Ancash of Quechua, Maparaju, the main peak, means "snowy mountain") is the highest mountain in the southern Peruvian Andes. Its summit measures 17,000 feet high. As a curious detail, if the measurement is made from the center of the Earth, it is the second highest mountain in the world after the Chimborazo volcano in Ecuador, almost two kilometers high, exceeding the height of Mount Everest.

This invitation from Antarel to their base there, brought to mind my old research contacts in Ancash, including the testimony of Vlado Kapetanovic and our first trip to the Andean region of Peru.

In my own research, I stumbled upon an interesting fact about the Huascarán that I had overlooked: In 2013, a team of Australian and German scientists revealed that the Huascarán is the place on the earth's surface where the gravitational force is the weakest.

In reaching this conclusion, the team of experts selected three billion locations on the planet, each equivalent to about 820 square feet, and processed them using a supercomputer. The process took about three weeks, where an average home PC would need about 475 years to complete the calculations.

The results showed that the place with "less gravity on earth" is Huascarán.

Considering that this Andean region was where the first case of contact with the Apunians was reported, the data seemed relevant.

What is really there?

A dream of the "future"

The message received in Buenos Aires triggered a series of synchronistic events that led us to plan a trip to the Huascarán National Park. Taking advantage of a visit to Lima in April, we would include a side trip to the Andean region. Initially, Alexander Szabo of Chile, Sol, and I embarked on this adventure. But in January 2015, after the extraordinary meeting for the world peace meditation on the outskirts of Capilla del Monte where around 1,000 people from about 22 countries participated, other companions joined: Raymundo Collazo, Fernando Lopez, Josep Tomas from Spain and Pablo Cascone from Argentina. All of us had already shared other experiences guided by the extraterrestrials.

After that meeting, I received a definitive confirmation in Buenos Aires.

The confirmation was an extraordinarily vivid dream.

In it, I saw myself with Antarel and a young woman, beautiful, with short blonde hair, who was about six feet tall. *"I introduce Ivika,"* said the Apunian. *"She is our current commander."*

It was in a very bright place, and I couldn't see well, but the mysterious Apunian woman was quick to explain:

"This is really happening. It is the contact that you are living with us. You are in our base at Huascarán."

I told them that I didn't understand, that I thought I was dreaming and at home in my bed.

"It's happening, but in another timeline that you would call the future," said Ivika. "Your dream is actually a holographic image that we are creating. This image is sent to your past as a mental image, while you are lying in your bedroom."

Puzzled, I asked why.

"It is so that when you arrive at your timeline in the meeting with us on April 12 in Yungay, you will be calmer because you will recognize that you have lived all this."

At that point, I woke up. Is it possible? I wondered again and again, trying to collect my thoughts. In talking with Sol, it became clear that this was no ordinary dream. It was indeed a message.

Unaware of what had happened to me, Fernando wrote from Mexico to tell me he had received a message for me, confirming a sighting. The extraterrestrials had told him that on April 12, in Yungay, they would take me to their base in Huascarán.

Ichic Puna

The flight from LC Peru aboard a small Bombardier Dash 8-202 with capacity for 37 passengers landed safely at Anta airport, just a 40-minute drive from the town of Yungay. I arrived in Yungay on April 10. We were happy to be there, at nearly 10,000 feet, amidst the beautiful mountains, many of them showing their superb snowy peaks.

With backpacks on our shoulders, we boarded a rented van to travel to Yungay. Our host on this journey to our hotel was Jorge Leon, a renowned mountain guide. We called upon his knowledge and asked if he knew of any open spaces next to our hotel in Yungay. Alejandro and I had had visions of a space nearby that had been marked by the extraterrestrials for the April 12 contact. We thought Jorge would know if such a place existed.

Ichic Puna was just such a place. It is an open field in the middle of the town, which features a huge rock.

We arrived at our hotel, the Rima Rima, in Yungay. It's a modest establishment, typical of the area, cozy and staffed by wonderful people. At the hotel, we found a large photograph of Ichic Puna in the reception hall.

A coincidence?

This was not a tourist place and yet, the sizeable photo and the rock dominated the main hall of the hotel. "You are going to tell me," he said, as he climbed the stairs to the third floor, heading to our room, "we should not take this as a confirmation. Wait."

When we opened the door to our room, Sol and I were amazed. On the wall facing the bed, there was a single frame with a photo of Ichic Puna.

Later, we found that every room in that hotel had the picture.

I knew that I needed to let go and be guided.

We visited Tobias Sarmiento, a co-worker and friend of Vlado Kapetanovic. As a result of what had happened to Vlado, Sarmiento had become an active investigator, who was also contacted by the Apunians. We chatted at length with him in his cozy house in Carhuaz. We agreed that contact with the Apunians had begun before the incident of Huallanca, in 1960.

The villagers of Callejón de Huaylas (the Alley of Huaylas) already knew about these things. The extraterrestrials were called "daddys" for their fatherly and protective behavior.

The first reports had come from nearby farms in the snowy area of Champará.

Champará mountain, sitting at almost 19,000 feet, is one of the many beautiful peaks in the White Range in Ancash. Kapetanovic cited the region as a place of first contact with the Apunians, after the incident of Huallanca. There were similar reports from the surrounding areas, Alpamayo, Huascarán and from the beautiful lagoons in Llanganuco. The people of this Andean paradise were quite accustomed to the presence of spaceships.

Even Jorge, our guide, showed us the place where, in 1967, the pictures of the so-called Ships of Yungay, had been taken. This case remains open and unexplained. Although we could not have access to the exact place where they would have taken those mysterious pictures, we saw it from a distance. It is located in an area of the Cordillera Negra (Black Range) where abundant eucalyptus trees are seen in one of the photos of the mentioned ships.

But our agenda held other things.

The Apunians had invited us to Llanganuco for the night of the 11th, as a preliminary step to the contact in Ichic Puna.

Ricardo González

Llanganuco: Another portal of contact

Llanganuco is one of the most beautiful places in Yungay and, according to the Apunians, a portal used for contact. There are two lagoons: *Chinancocha* meaning "female lagoon" and *Orcococha* or "male lagoon." They are formed from the runoff of the emblematic peaks of Ancash, Huascarán and Huandoy. Chinancocha, the place we chose for our work on the night of the 11th, is 4700 feet long, 4 and half miles wide and 90 feet deep. We settled on its shores, near some cattails (aqua plant) and *queñual* trees (Polylepis Pauta, the typical tree of Peru).

In Yungay, we had been cautioned that the weather in Llanganuco was bad and it was suggested that we not go there. The National Weather Service announced intense rains in the region and even hail.

Not only did it not rain, but there was a beautiful clear sky that allowed us to enjoy the full canopy of stars and the snowy peaks, which resembled giant guardians.

There was no one there, possibly because of the weather reports. No tourists or backpackers, perhaps frightened away by the aforementioned meteorological forecast. The night was beautiful, but also very strange.

Our electronic gadgets began to fail in Llanganuco. First, it was Fernando's night vision camera—the batteries ran out three times. Then, the Nikon P510 camera operated by Josep. Even my flashlights failed. The astronomical laser we use to indicate any anomalous object in the sky, stopped working. What was happening? Was it the Andean cold at this altitude? Then, we knew that it was not. Upon returning to the hotel, the camera equipment began working. The batteries were fine.

All of this coincided with a light that emerged across the lagoon. It was not any kind of reflection. We observed an object that shot out from behind one of the snowy ranges that flew in a winding path above us.

Moments later, I received the following message:

Yes, we are close. I am Ivika. I am in our base of Huascarán. We have been monitoring you from here. You already know that we always accompany you, but be aware of our limitations and your learning that causes you doubts. By following our invitation, you have set up something important. You will know more tomorrow.

Coming to Llanganuco was a test and preparation. You saw us, but do not expect to capture our demonstrations. We understand that this constitutes an important element for your corroboration and evidence for others and, for that reason, we have allowed it in the past. But now you should be concentrating on the invitation, and maintain the suggested preparation.

Remember the number 55 is an activating key to this stage of contact with us.

The place identified (Ichic Puna), is correct. Be there at 5:00 pm. You will know at what point to move closer to the rock. Come alone. That stone will be activated as a door leading down to us. Your colleagues, at a distance, will support you and they will experience what is appropriate for them. Their bodies have been aligned with powerful energies. We have been working with you here. They have felt it and it is part of the purpose of the appointment in Llanganuco.

Come with confidence. We have confidence in you and everything you are doing.

Come closer to us,
Ivika

Contact From Planet Apu

Chapter 11

Ivika's Message

April 12, 2015. What to say? How can I explain the complexity of my feelings as I approached the Ichic Puna group on that unforgettable day? I was more than excited for this next contact.

Yungay had been rebuilt after the earthquake, although it was far from what it had been before. It was located in a safer area, which seemed quiet that afternoon with a partly cloudy sky that hid Huascarán.

Our walk was brief, as Ichic Puna is located in the middle of the village, in a field surrounded by farmland and modest homes. Not far away are immense local TV antennas. That is, we were not far from civilization. I wondered why the extraterrestrials had scheduled a direct contact here? Ichic Puna had a special atmosphere. It was a natural gathering place. Everything was centered around the huge stone, planted in the ground at a slight incline. This would be where the contact would occur.

Due to its elevation, Ichic Puna (in Quechua, small puna) offers a beautiful view of the valley and mountains.

We chose a group of rocks to sit on and waited for contact. Ivika had said that I would know the exact moment when I was to get close to the rock. We meditated while we waited for that moment.

Around 6:00 pm, I instinctively stood up and walked slowly, toward the stone. It was a little more than 300 feet away and I saw nothing unusual. The whole area looked normal.

When I reached the stone on its slightly elevated site, nothing looked out of the ordinary, although I had a strong feeling of being watched. I decided to touch the stone to see if I would feel anything, attempting to figure out the next step.

I detected something strange.

The stone was very hot, as hot as an iron. The heat forced me to take my hands off the surface for a second. It did not, however, burn my hands. They were not even hot from touching the stone.

I decided to touch it again and, in spite of the heat, left my hands there. Soon, I got used to the sensation. I felt a strange energy pulsating, similar to a human heartbeat. I put my forehead against the huge stone, which seemed to be alive.

It was in that moment that the upright rock of Ichic Puna "swallowed" me. I seemed to have entered into it. An intense bluish-white light flooded everything.

I found myself standing in a large lighted structure, composed of strange geometric forms. Despite being different from each other, they formed a coherent and harmonious space. In the midst of my surprise and my rapid breathing and indescribable thrill, the light became less bright and I could distinguish three beings standing in front of me.

"Welcome to our Huascarán base," said one of these figures.

The middle of these three beings was a woman, the woman I had seen in my dream.

Ricardo González

The Minius

Ivika was a young woman by appearance and very human looking, although with slightly stylized facial features. She stood in front of me and on her left was Antarel. The giant Apunian was dressed in his regular metallic gray color. Ivika wore a kind of uniform as well. On her suit I saw a symbol that reminded me of a trident.

To the right of Ivika, but a bit apart, stood another woman wearing the gray uniform. On each, their hands and faces were exposed. This *guide* was a little shorter than Ivika. She appeared to be about 5 foot, 9 inches tall. She also looked young, between 25 and 30 years of age and had long, shoulder-length brown hair. She was holding a cube in her left hand, which was lit with a bluish-white light, like the glow that had drawn me there.

"Her name is Aimana," Ivika said. "We see that the object attracts you."

"Yes," I said. "I have seen that cube in other experiences with you."

"In your world they are known as the tesseract.[1] We use that term so you can understand. We have brought you here with it."

How was that possible? And why to the rock in Ichic Puna?

"Am I physically here?" I asked hastily.

---

[1] The term "tesseract" was first coined in 1888 by the English mathematician Charles Howard Hinton. In geometry, the tesseract is the four-dimensional analog of the cube; the tesseract is to the cube as the cube is to the square. Just as the surface of the cube consists of six square faces, the hypersurface of the tesseract consists of eight cubical cells. The tesseract is one of the six convex regular 4-polytopes. Obviously, we cannot see that "hypercube" in the fourth dimension, since only the points that touch our universe would be visible, so hopefully we would see a "common cube" only in the event that the hypercube touched 3D space in parallel relationship one of its sides.

Ivika motioned to Aimana with her right hand. The cube began to illuminate a bit more and projected an extraordinarily real image, in which I saw myself still standing at the Ichic Puna Rock, with my hands and forehead leaning against it.

"My body is in Ichic Puna and I am mentally projected here?" I questioned, as I watched, engrossed with the image.

"You are in both places at once," Ivika said. "However, your consciousness is only active here with us in this experience. You should not be surprised. We conducted a similar test with you at Mount Shasta. The goal is to become familiar with the multiplicity of realities in which we operate.

"We chose Ichic Puna," Ivika continued, "after a study that we conducted in the area. We were looking for a place close to your location where we could connect with the natural power lines of Huascarán. We used this network through the tesseract to bring you here."

"I have several questions," I told the extraterrestrial woman, while Antarel watched in silence. "Is this experience connected to what you began to reveal to me in 2001? With the human projects and travel to Alpha Centauri? Were you trying to say that you are humans coming from the future?"

"No, we are not human," answered Ivika. "To you, we are extraterrestrials, because we were not born on Earth. But, some of us are closely linked to humankind because we are, to some extent, your descendants."

"I don't understand," I said perplexed.

"See for yourself," she said.

Once again, the tesseract began to glow and project a picture of the Earth. I felt I was seeing the future. In the scene, I saw that our world had developed accentuated problems of coexistence resulting in wars, famine and inequality. I could see huge masses of people wandering in a clear picture of global overpopulation. There were scenes of chaos and despair. Then, the image changed and I saw a major scientific facility in a place I knew to be the Atacama Desert, in Chile. It was a launch pad for spaceships. A huge corporation, under the auspices of the United Nations, had created a space project to travel to a world they hoped to terraform, which was located in the Alpha Centauri star system.

Most disturbing was to see that the astronauts were children.

Hundreds of boys, between 12 and 15 years old, I estimate, had been trained in psychic abilities and scientific knowledge for the big trip. According to my vision, this will happen in the distant future, beyond our current generation.

"That trip was made possible by the Minius[2]," explained Ivika. "It is the most powerful source behind the illusion of material energy. Those spaceships that you see will have a hybrid technology, which combines with the power of Minius to shorten space travel. Humanity will begin to enter the knowledge of dimensional folds and other realities in the cosmos."

"And what happened?"

"Keep watching," Ivika said.

The tesseract showed me another scene. Something happened to those ships as they traveled through space to Alpha Centauri. During the trip, a phenomenon linked to the Minius and folds [in space-time] made the ships arrive at an alternate reality, reaching Alpha Centauri, but in the past. The child astronauts lost their memory due to the incident.

Upon arrival at that planet, somewhere near Alpha Centauri, they were greeted by human-looking extraterrestrials who had already colonized it. These beings, ancestors of Antarel, rescued

---

[2]This term had already been used by the Apunians during contact with Vlado Kapetanovic.

the human space expedition and integrated them into their culture.

In the first stage, they showed me—and helped me understand through the tesseract—the extraterrestrials did not immediately reveal their human origin or anything about the failed space mission. For many reasons, from psychological to scientific, they felt it was not the time.

The human spacecraft carried two important files, a super memory, which consisted of a record of the entire history of the Earth, human inventions, art, early civilizations, all available data on the evolution of man; and a second file called super seed, a real vault with millions of genetic samples from nearly all forms of life on Earth.

In addition, on the spaceships there were numerous robots and advanced computers with construction capacity, all available to the young scientist astronauts to terraform a new home in the Alpha Centauri star system. The Apunians kept all this in quarantine until the hundreds of terrestrial cosmonauts could adapt to their new situation.

And so, over time, there was a mix between humans and Apunians—the descendants of this union and custodians of the truth.

Those *mestizos*, people of mixed race, had access to all the information from the spaceships of their earthly ancestors and made a decision to return to Earth to prevent humanity from going through the crisis that precipitated the trip.

The *mestizos* considered that, beyond the survival of the human species, the circumstances that required their ancestors to leave earth was the consequence of neglecting healthy living on a planet that was once a haven of beauty and resources.

The Apunians identified with the earthly travelers. They, too, had lost their home world, which led them to colonize the planet Apu in the Alpha Centauri system. Thus, the extraterrestrials and the mixed-race extraterrestrial/human descendants devised a project to send a mission to the past of the Earth and alert human beings.

The particular dimensional situation of the Earth that I mentioned earlier as the Cosmic Plan, allowed the Apunians to make a trip to the past, but they could not act alone. (Later, they would be integrated into the agenda of the so-called Galactic Confederation to aid the planet in all types of missions.)0

After this latest vision, the tesseract turned off.

"All of this occurred in another timeline outside your current perception," Ivika explained. "We are aware that this is very difficult for a creature that usually moves in a three-dimensional plane of consciousness to understand. What has been shown to you belongs to what you would call the future and is the beginning of the origin of some of us."

"Why are you telling us now?" I asked.

"Several scientists of your world have received our messages and warnings about what you have seen," Ivika stated firmly. "Not all of them have been sensitized to this knowledge. Then, we noticed the progress being made by scientists on earth with the big particle accelerator, which is prior to the discovery of the Minius power, and we decided it was time."

Aimana then lifted the tesseract for me to see, while Ivika added, "The tesseract does not have the power, but the Minius does."

Without further hesitation, I approached the mysterious cube trying to see inside.

"You cannot see the Minius. It is infinitely small and infinitely powerful. The tesseract only contains it," Antarel explained.

"We will be one..."

"This experience," continued the giant Apunian, "is an important evaluation for us and determines the next steps. We want to see if you can assimilate this information to move to a second stage of the revelations."

"When will the second stage of revelations occur?" I asked.

"If the conditions are met, then at the meeting suggested in Atacama," Ivika responded.

My mind was trying to sort through all this. It had been fourteen years since Antarel had told me the first part of the story. A story that I could not have begun to imagine.

"The message is that you must follow the set path," Antarel went on to say. "We told you in the contact at Mount Shasta that the transition from Earth to a higher reality was insured, as is the beginning of the awakening of humanity; but you have to maintain conscious awareness and balance in your actions.

"Keep in mind," he said, "that you are living at a crucial time to make decisions. Everything that man decides in the coming years will influence his future. It is the final major step for the re-dimensioning."

"Now you will begin to understand," said Ivika, "that beyond contact with you, we are also connecting with your descendants and with all the people who are touching these messages in order to generate a chain reaction in the future. We are not only special travelers, but also travelers of time, so we cannot act too freely on Earth, or with witnesses, with specific exceptions, as any wrong move on our part could create dangerous paradoxes."

"Our mission has involved many stages," Antarel interjected, "beginning with our involvement in human culture at different times, living like you, learning and observing. Our laboratory base here in Huascarán is actually a spaceship, the first to arrive for this project. And, as you know, we have other similar facilities in several mountainous areas of your world.

"After World War II and the atomic explosions in Japan," continued Antarel, "we began to contact the inhabitants of the Andean region. They were important to us. While other human beings faced war, men from here cultivated the field, loved the mountains and the sun. Vlado had contact with us afterwards. And, as you will understand, it was an important link in our anthropological study, since he had been a soldier in that war; a soldier by circumstance, a soldier who suffered human pain and who loved these mountains as well as the local people."

"We tried to avoid the disaster in Yungay," Ivika added. "But we were very limited in our actions, and our warnings were not heard. Human behavior has been detrimental to the balance of the planet and it can be seen in this region. It is therefore possible that other destructive events will be generated in the future. We are doing all that is possible. But remember that you have the key to change all things."

"Ivika, are you a *mestizo*?" I asked on impulse, in the midst of this conversation.

"Aimana and I are," she answered.

Deeply moved, I tried to control myself to ask them an important question.

"If we change the 'future history' in caring for the planet and with peaceful coexistence, it means that space travel to Alpha Centauri would never...I mean, some of you would cease to exist in that timeline."

"Brother," Ivika said to me, with an immeasurable peace, "you will understand that nothing in the universe disappears, it only transforms itself. We will be one."

"We will be one," said Antarel.

Then, they departed, but first they gave me some personal messages.

Ivika told me that all kinds of news would happen in the scientific community relating to what they had revealed to me. And so it will occur.

A new glow was emitted by the tesseract, which Aimana operated silently, and I found myself back in Ichic Puna.

I felt dizzy, as if two people trying to integrate into one.

I went to meet the group, and there I shared this extraordinary experience and its powerful message.

Above: Drawing of Ivika by Ramiro Rossi.

Contact From Planet Apu

Epilogue

Time

There were some follow-up details to this contact—really curious facts—that puzzled us.

Back at the hotel, Fernando told us that all the data from the memory card of his night vision equipment had been deleted. He couldn't explain how, but it happened when he was trying to download the contents of the card onto the computer. It was strange. We tried to rescue everything that was filmed, but in vain.

He was not able to restore, from the memory card, the sighting in Llanganuco that he captured, nor the video of my experience at Ichic Puna Rock. Interestingly, immediately after the sighting in Llanganuco, the video of the UFO was perfectly reproduced in the display of his camera. We couldn't see any problems in any of the other cameras and, yet, after Ichic Puna all of the archives were erased.

Ivika anticipated this, López reminded us. In the message of Llanganuco, she warned us not to be waiting for their manifestation.

But something had been recorded from that unforgettable contact in Ichic Puna. Sol took a picture of me, when I was returning from the rock after the contact. The image, which we could see, when we returned to the hotel, left us all surprised.

It was like a wink from the extraterrestrials.

In this photograph taken in automatic mode, I looked, indeed, as if I was walking amidst the weeds of Ichic Puna. However, my image was duplicated, as if I were two distinct people.

My rational mind wanted to see that image as a typical blurred picture. In fact, I want to keep seeing it as such, but there it was on film.

Was the photo random or not? Did they want a blurred picture to represent exactly what had happened, and what I had just narrated to the group prior to viewing the pictures? In fact, as soon as I met the group in Ichic Puna, immediately following the contact, I narrated and recorded the experience in audio, so as not to lose any details of the message.

As I say, that picture confused us. Either way, it's not necessary to have a photograph of this event. The contact was real and convincing.

Later, I showed it two professional photographers, and they thought it was very bizarre, because I am separated from the other Ricardo, so to speak. Sol took the picture in automatic, not in exhibition mode. I was moving when the picture was shot, walking very slowly. Given that, the photographers told me that it would be expected the picture of me would look double or blurry, but my images wouldn't be so separated and have such clear definition and this is a digital camera. We have used this camera for two years, taking all kinds of pictures throughout the world, never has such a thing happened.

As it was, whether or not a technical explanation is possible, that photograph is an extraordinary message. It is certainly one way to remember—to never forget—what the tesseract showed me.

In the Yungay hotel, shortly before our flight to Lima, Jorge gave us more details about Ichic Puna. A prestigious Colombian archaeologist, Alexander Herrera Wassilowsky, had visited and studied the place. She was led to hypothesize that the rock had been placed, since it is aligned at certain times of the year with the sunrise from the summit of Huascarán. According to Jorge, it is believed that in the past, Ichic Puna may have been a place where solstices and equinoxes were observed and celebrated.

On April 17, just five days after my contact in Yungay, I was interviewed by the Mexican journalist, Yohanan Diaz. I shared the message of the Apunians, including one event in the future in which human space travel to Alpha Centauri will occur. The interview is available on YouTube.

Two weeks later, the news reported the findings of a group of scientists from the University of California. In the report, scientists warned that astronauts could lose their memory and cognitive capacities when exposed to cosmic radiation in deep space.

Days later, NASA revealed the design of a spacecraft with warp velocity. This advancement would propel a manned spacecraft to a speed equal to several multiples of the speed of light, while avoiding the problems associated with the relativistic time dilation. This type of propulsion is based on bent or distorted space-time and works in such a way as to enable the spaceship to be closer to its destination.

According to statements by physicist Harold White, who is in charge of this project, it is theoretically and practically possible to achieve a driving force to enable a spaceship to get to Alpha Centauri in just two weeks, as measured by the time elapsed on Earth.

The Apunians were right. At this time in our history, important decisions are being made about the future of our race.

Interestingly, the human journey to Alpha Centauri is being carried out from a facility in the Atacama region in Chile, precisely in the area where La Silla Observatory is located. Its facilities house one of the world's most modern spectrographs, the High Accuracy Radial Velocity Planet Searcher (HARPS), which aims to observe extra solar planets. As I mentioned, it was precisely this observatory that found the planet next to the star Alpha Centauri B.

Since I shared my testimony, people who follow my work and other researchers have been sending me all kinds of information that help make sense of the Apunians' story, from the latest developments of the LHC (CERN's Large Hadron Collider particle accelerator), to declarations of the Russian cosmonaut Alexei Leonov, the man who made the first space walk on March 18, 1965, who said in recent interviews that highly trained children should be sent in future space travels.

All this information is available and can be quickly confirmed with a simple web search.

Time is one of the keys to understanding all this.

So, then, what is reality? How does the present, past and future function? At what point in our existence do the distinct possibilities connect in the universe?

These questions are impossible to answer.

However, through this contact experience with the Apunians, I was left with a clear belief that we have the capacity to change things, if we are conscious of the situation.

If, from our point of perception in space-time, we choose the right path, which is based on love and service, that force will be replicated, as a sort of fractal projection to the whole cosmic fabric.

There are many other matters that are difficult for the mind to understand and, yet, there are some that the heart will recognize.

I know that the message will reach those who need to receive it.

We are not alone.

And, we are them.

Ricardo González
Buenos Aires
May 24, 2015

"The Double..."

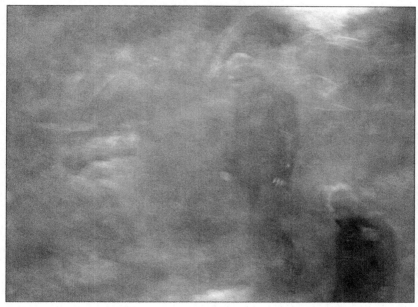

Above: The mysterious picture of Ichic Puna. Just a blurred picture? A whim of fate? Or, no matter the explanation, a message from *them*?

Contact From Planet Apu

"Everything for others..."
Apunian Message

Contact From Planet Apu

Made in the USA
Monee, IL
24 June 2020